FEARFUL AVOIDANT
ATTACHMENT HEALING
BREAKTHROUGH

Practical Strategies to Break Cycles of Fear, Build Emotional Security, and Reclaim Your Authentic Self with Proven Methods for Nurturing Lasting, Trust-Filled Relationships

JOHN C. ROOSEVELT

COPYRIGHT NOTICE

DISCLAIMER

The information in Anxious Attachment Transformation is for educational purposes, based on the author's research and experience. It does not replace professional mental health advice. The author and publisher do not guarantee accuracy or assume liability for any actions taken. Readers should consult qualified professionals for personal concerns.

TABLE OF CONTENT

INTRODUCTION

Understanding Your Attachment Style

We all have this deep need for connection, but for many of us, relationships can feel more like a source of anxiety rather than security. If you have ever found yourself in a place where love feels complicated, where the very relationships you cherish seem to stir up fear or uncertainty, it might have more to do with your attachment style than you realize.

From a young age, we develop attachment styles based on how we were cared for and the connections we formed with those around us. These early bonds shape how we experience love, closeness, and even conflict. If you find yourself longing for intimacy but feeling afraid of getting too close, it is possible you have a fearful avoidant attachment style. This style makes relationships feel like a constant balancing act craving connection while feeling compelled to protect yourself by pushing others away.

This push-and-pull behavior can feel exhausting, not just for you, but for those you care about. And here's the thing,most of us live our lives without ever recognizing these patterns for what they are. We repeat them, often unaware of the underlying fear and confusion that keep us stuck. But awareness is the key to breaking these cycles.

Once you start to understand your attachment style, you can begin to see the fear that's been driving your behavior. And this awareness opens the door to change. This book is designed to support you in making that shift. It offers more than a collection of strategies.This book is designed to support you in making that shift. It offers more than a collection of strategies.. It's about learning to heal those old wounds and rediscover the parts of yourself that have been buried under layers of fear. As you do, you'll find a way to build deeper, more secure relationships, ones that are based on love and trust, not fear.

*Emotional freedom is something everyone deserves,
and it's within your reach. Emotional freedom is about
being able to connect with others without the constant
fear of rejection, or the worry that love will end in
pain. For someone with a fearful avoidant attachment
style, the idea of being emotionally free might feel
impossible. But trust me it isn't.*

*Emotional freedom does not mean erasing fear
completely. Fear is a part of life, and it will always be
there in some form. The difference is that when you are
emotionally free, fear no longer has the power to
control your actions or define your relationships.
Instead of letting fear keep you at arm's length from
the people you care about, you will learn how to
manage it, make space for trust, and let yourself be
vulnerable **in** healthy ways.*

This book is going to guide you through the process of
getting there. You'll start to see the patterns you've been
stuck in, and you'll learn step-by-step how to change
them. As you read, you will begin to recognize the
fear-based reactions that have been driving your
behavior, and more importantly, how to move toward
healthier, more secure ways of relating.

Fearful avoidant attachment impacts so much more than
just romantic relationships. It can affect every part of
your life, how you connect with friends, how you relate

to your family, and even how you approach work or other social situations. You might notice that it's difficult to fully trust others, or that asking for help feels impossible because deep down, you fear being let down or rejected. This often leads to a sense of isolation, even when you are surrounded by people who care about you.

The good news is, you are not stuck in this pattern forever. Your attachment style is something that was shaped by your experiences, and with the right tools, it can be changed. This book is going to show you how to break free from the cycle of fear and avoidance that has kept you from feeling safe and loved in your relationships.

Here's what you can expect to learn as we walk through this journey together:

You will understand how your fearful avoidant attachment style developed in the first place. This understanding is the foundation of your healing process. Once you see where it came from, it becomes easier to change.

You will learn specific techniques to break the cycle of fear that's been keeping you stuck. Fear is often at the root of avoidant attachment, and we'll go through practical, proven ways to manage and reduce that fear so you can start to feel secure in your relationships.

You will discover strategies for building emotional security. Emotional security is essential for creating healthy, fulfilling relationships, and you will gain tools to help you build that security within yourself and with others.

You will stop self-sabotaging. So many people with fearful avoidant attachment find themselves unknowingly sabotaging their relationships, pushing people away because of fear. We will talk about how to recognize these behaviors and how to stop them before they cause harm.

You will learn how to nurture trust-filled relationships. Trust is a crucial part of any relationship, but it can feel especially challenging for those who struggle with attachment issues. Together, we will explore how to build and sustain trust with others, even if it's something you've struggled with in the past.

You will reconnect with your authentic self. Fearful avoidant attachment can make it difficult to show your true self, leaving parts of you hidden or suppressed out of fear of rejection. We will go through how to reconnect with your true self and how to express your needs with confidence and honesty.

Each step you take will bring you closer to a more secure attachment style. You will begin to notice changes not just in how you relate to others, but in how you relate to yourself. This journey is about more than just improving your relationships with the people in your life, it's about creating a relationship with yourself that is full of love, compassion, and understanding.

CHAPTER 1

Recognizing the Signs of Fearful Avoidant Attachment

Let's start with a simple truth: many of us have patterns that we follow in relationships without ever being fully aware of them. These patterns run in the background, shaping how we connect, love, and trust. They were formed long ago, often before we even knew what love or trust truly meant. For those with fearful avoidant attachment, the struggle is deep. There's this ongoing inner conflict, one that pulls you in opposite directions. You want connection, but you also fear it. You crave love, but you're terrified of being hurt. The push and pull create confusion and leave you feeling emotionally drained. But once you recognize the signs of this attachment style, you can begin to break free. It's time to move from fear to freedom, from insecurity to trust.

Early Signs You May Have Missed

Fearful avoidant attachment doesn't announce itself with obvious signals. It's subtle and often masked by behaviors that seem normal. You might have missed the signs, thinking that your reactions are just "the way you are." But the truth is, these behaviors stem from a deeper, often hidden place. They're not the real you,they're the version of you shaped by fear.

Think back to your past relationships. Have you ever found yourself deeply invested in someone, only to pull away when things started to feel serious? Or maybe you've felt a surge of panic when a partner or close friend got too emotionally close. This fear of intimacy doesn't mean you don't want love. In fact, you probably want it desperately, but there's a part of you that sees closeness as a threat.

One of the key signs of fearful avoidant attachment is this paradox: the intense longing for connection, combined with an equally intense fear of being hurt or rejected. It creates an emotional dance coming close, but never quite letting yourself fully engage.

Another early sign is the tendency to distrust others, even those who've done nothing to earn that distrust. You may find yourself constantly questioning people's motives, wondering if they're going to leave you or betray you. This constant state of hypervigilance can make it difficult to relax in relationships. You're always on edge, waiting for the other shoe to drop, even if there's no reason for it to do so.

Then there's self-sabotage, something many people with fearful avoidant attachment experience but don't always recognize. Maybe you've ended relationships that were actually going well, or you've pushed people away when they've tried to get close. You might find yourself picking fights over small things, or becoming distant when someone shows genuine care. It's as if you're testing their love, waiting to see if they'll stick around despite the obstacles you throw in their way.

These are just a few of the early signs, but recognizing them is the first step toward healing. Awareness is the foundation of change. Once you see the patterns, you can begin to unravel them.

How Attachment Patterns Develop Over Time

Understanding how your fearful avoidant attachment style developed is crucial. You weren't born with these patterns,they were learned, and like anything learned, they can be unlearned. But to do that, we need to go back to the source: childhood.

In the early years of life, we form bonds with our primary caregivers,usually our parents. These bonds create the blueprint for how we understand relationships. If those early bonds were inconsistent, where love and care were unpredictable, it can create a sense of instability within us. Perhaps your caregivers were emotionally unavailable, or maybe they were loving one moment and distant the next. This inconsistency teaches a child one thing: relationships are unsafe.

Imagine a young child who reaches out for comfort but is met with unpredictability,sometimes they receive warmth, other times they're ignored. Over time, this child learns that closeness is dangerous. The fear of being rejected or abandoned takes root, and as that child grows, those same fears follow them into adulthood.

Fearful avoidant attachment is often the result of these mixed signals from caregivers. You want love, but you've learned that love isn't always safe. You've come to expect that people will leave or betray you, so you protect yourself by keeping a certain distance, even from those who genuinely care about you.

But here's the key thing to understand: your attachment style is not your destiny. It's a set of behaviors you learned as a way to survive emotionally in your early years. And while those behaviors may have served you then, they don't have to define your life now. You can rewire these patterns, creating new, healthier ways of connecting with others.

Self-Assessment of Your Attachment Style

It's one thing to read about fearful avoidant attachment, but it's another to truly see how it plays out in your own life. To begin the process of healing, you need to know where you stand. This self-assessment will help you get a clearer picture of your attachment style and how it's been influencing your relationships.

Take a moment to reflect on the following questions:

1. When you think about getting close to someone emotionally, what's your first reaction? Is it excitement, or does it come with a sense of fear or anxiety?
2. Do you find yourself pulling away when someone tries to get close, even if it's someone you deeply care about?
3. In past relationships, have you noticed a pattern of pushing people away just when things start to get serious or emotionally intense?
4. Do you often worry that the people in your life partners, friends, family,might leave you, even if they've given no indication that they will?
5. Are you more comfortable when there's some emotional distance between you and others? Do you feel safer when you're not too vulnerable?

6. Have you ever sabotaged a relationship, either consciously or unconsciously, because you were afraid of getting hurt?
7. Do you struggle with trusting others, even those who have been consistently kind and supportive?
8. When conflict arises in a relationship, is your instinct to pull away or shut down emotionally?

As you think through these questions, try to be as honest with yourself as possible. If you find that several of these questions resonate with you, there's a good chance that you're operating from a place of fearful avoidant attachment. But here's the empowering part: this awareness is your starting point. You're not stuck in this pattern. Recognizing these behaviors is the first step toward changing them.

> *We all have moments when fear takes over when the thought of being truly vulnerable feels too risky. But remember this: you are worthy of love and connection. The fear you feel is not a reflection of your value; it's simply a learned response. As you move forward, know that it's possible to break free from the chains of fearful avoidant attachment. You can learn to trust, to love deeply, and to feel safe in your relationships.*

This journey isn't about becoming someone else. It's about rediscovering the real you the version of you that isn't driven by fear or guardedness. The version of you that is open to love, to connection, and to the kind of relationships you've always wanted. With each step you take, you're moving closer to emotional freedom, where fear no longer has the power to hold you back. You're capable of change, and that change starts now.

CHAPTER 2

The Emotional Cost of Fear

There is a weight you have been carrying for so long that it might even feel like it is part of you. This weight comes from living with a fearful avoidant attachment style a deep-rooted fear that has quietly chipped away at your peace of mind. The toll it takes on your mental health is real, though it is often hidden from even your own awareness.

The truth is, when you are caught in cycles of fear, your mind can become a prison. Fearful avoidant attachment weaves uncertainty and mistrust into the very fabric of how you think, how you interact, and how you perceive the world around you. And while you may have learned to live with this constant push and pull, the impact on your mental health is not something to be brushed aside. It's there, manifesting as anxiety, stress, and emotional exhaustion, leaving you drained.

You are not alone in feeling this way. For many people with fearful avoidant attachment, the mental and emotional toll goes unnoticed until it becomes overwhelming. But let's be clear: this is not who you are. This is a reflection of what you have been carrying. And now, by recognizing it, you can start the process of setting yourself free.

How Fear Shapes Your Mind

Fearful avoidant attachment has a unique way of shaping your thoughts. The fear of rejection, the fear of getting too close, the fear of being abandoned,these fears are the driving force behind your mental patterns. They quietly dictate how you respond to others and, more importantly, how you view yourself.

Let's talk about your inner dialogue. Those subtle but persistent thoughts that run in the background, the ones that question your worth, your place in the world, and your right to be loved. They often sound something like this:

- *"What if they don't really love me?"*
- *"They'll leave eventually, so why should I let myself get attached?"*
- *"I can't trust anyone to stay, so I need to protect myself."*

These thoughts seem harmless at first glance, but over time, they become the foundation for how you engage in relationships. The fear-based thinking leads you to question the sincerity of others, doubt the love you receive, and hold yourself back from the vulnerability that relationships require. Even in moments of joy or closeness, there's a nagging voice that whispers, "This won't last." And with that voice comes the constant tension that makes it hard to fully relax into relationships or even into your own sense of self.

The Invisible Impact on Mental Health
The impact of living with this attachment style goes beyond just how you relate to others. It can create a sense of ongoing unease that affects every part of your life, leaving you feeling emotionally and mentally depleted.

First, let's talk about anxiety. Fearful avoidant attachment often leads to high levels of anxiety, especially in relationships. This isn't always the kind of anxiety that makes you visibly panicked; it's more subtle. It shows up in the form of overthinking, constantly second-guessing yourself, or trying to anticipate what might go wrong. You might find yourself replaying conversations, analyzing what you said or what someone else said, wondering if you misstepped. This mental replay can become exhausting, leaving little space for you to simply be present.

Then there's the emotional exhaustion that comes from keeping people at arm's length, even though you desperately crave closeness. The constant cycle of pushing people away, then pulling them back in, wears you down. It's a cycle that feeds your insecurities and leaves you questioning your own worth. Over time, this creates a deep sense of emotional fatigue. You're constantly trying to navigate a maze of fear, and that in itself is draining.

The weight of mistrust, too, should not be underestimated. When you live in fear that those around you will hurt you or leave you, it's difficult to feel at peace. Your mind stays in a hypervigilant state, always looking for signs of betrayal or rejection. And this mental state often translates into physical tension, tight shoulders, shallow breathing, restlessness.

This combination of anxiety, emotional exhaustion, and constant mistrust can lead to more serious mental health challenges like depression. You may not even realize it's happening, because it often unfolds slowly over time. One day you might wake up and realize that you've been feeling numb for months, that joy feels distant, and that hope feels harder to hold onto.

Breaking Free: A Path to Mental Clarity

Now, here is the part where things can begin to change. The first step toward reclaiming your mental health is awareness. By shining a light on the hidden toll that fearful avoidant attachment has taken on you, you are already starting to reclaim control. Recognizing how your thoughts and feelings have been shaped by fear opens the door to healing.

You don't have to live under the weight of constant worry. You don't have to keep protecting yourself from the very thing you want the most: connection. Healing begins with shifting how you relate to your own thoughts, and with time, how you relate to others.

Journaling to Identify Fear-Based Thoughts

Journaling is one of the most powerful tools you can use to bring awareness to your thoughts. It offers a space where you can be honest with yourself, without judgment. When you take the time to put your thoughts on paper, patterns start to emerge, and you can see more clearly what's been driving your emotions and actions.

Here's how you can start:

- **Step 1: Set aside time to write**

Find a quiet space where you won't be interrupted for at least 15-20 minutes. This is your time to be with your thoughts, so make sure you feel comfortable and calm.

- **Step 2: Ask yourself specific questions**

The goal here is to uncover the fear-based thoughts that are affecting your mental health. Below are some questions to help guide you:

- *What are the fears that come up when I think about getting close to someone?*
- *When someone shows me love or affection, what thoughts or doubts immediately pop into my mind?*
- *Do I find myself assuming that relationships will end in rejection or abandonment? If so, where do these thoughts come from?*
- *How do I feel when I think about trusting others? What makes it difficult for me to trust?*
- *Are there moments when I feel the need to push people away, even though I don't want to be alone?*

Write down whatever comes to mind, without censoring yourself. This is your space to explore.

- **Step 3: Look for patterns**

After you've written for a while, take a step back and read through what you've written. Are there recurring themes or fears that show up? Do you notice certain triggers that make you feel more vulnerable or fearful? These patterns are clues to what is driving your attachment style.

- **Step 4: Challenge those thoughts**

Once you've identified the fear-based thoughts, it's time to gently challenge them. Ask yourself:

- *Are these fears based on actual experiences, or are they projections of past hurts?*
- *What evidence do I have that people in my life are trustworthy?*
- *Am I confusing past relationships with my current ones?*
- *What would my life look like if I chose to trust more and fear less?*
- *Challenging your thoughts doesn't mean dismissing them. It means questioning whether they are serving you or holding you back. This process helps you start breaking down the barriers that fear has built around you.*

Moving Forward with Greater Awareness

By now, you've started to uncover some of the hidden thoughts that have been impacting your mental health. This exercise is just the beginning. The more you become aware of these fear-based patterns, the more power you will have to change them.

Your mind doesn't have to be a battlefield. You deserve peace. You deserve relationships where fear is not the dominant force. Journaling will be one of your greatest allies in this journey,it will help you notice your thoughts, understand them, and eventually shift them.

With time, you'll find that the fears that once held you captive no longer have the same power over you. They might still show up, but now you'll recognize them for what they are: remnants of old wounds, not reflections of your current reality. Healing is not about erasing the past; it's about learning to live beyond it.

The mind is resilient, and so are you. As you continue this journey, keep reminding yourself that you are not defined by fear. You are capable of building a life that is driven by love, trust, and emotional freedom. And every time you sit down to journal, you are taking one more step toward that reality.

CHAPTER 3

Understanding the Roots of Avoidance

When we think about why we struggle to form deep, trusting relationships, we often look at the present the behaviors we see in ourselves now. But to truly understand why you have developed a fearful avoidant attachment style, you need to look back. The roots of avoidance often trace back to childhood experiences that shaped the way you see relationships, connection, and even yourself. These early patterns, though often subtle, can leave a lasting mark, creating a fear of rejection and intimacy that echoes into adulthood.

Every child craves love and security, but not every child receives it in the way they need. If your early experiences with caregivers were unpredictable, inconsistent, or even emotionally unavailable, you likely learned early on that relationships were something to be wary of. The very people meant to provide you with love and protection may have left you feeling unsure, anxious, or fearful. And as a result, you developed ways to protect yourself in ways that, over time, became avoidance.

The avoidance you feel now, the hesitation to let people in, is not something you chose. It's something you learned. But now, as an adult, you have the power to unlearn it. You can begin to understand why you've been afraid of intimacy and why rejection feels like such a looming threat. By understanding these roots, you can begin to heal them.

The Role of Childhood Experiences

Our childhood experiences are like the soil in which the seeds of our emotional patterns are planted. The way we were cared for, the love we received,or didn't receive shaped the foundation for how we connect with others today. If you grew up with caregivers who were emotionally unavailable, unpredictable, or neglectful, you may have learned that closeness was something to be feared rather than embraced.

Think back to your earliest memories of care. Were your caregivers consistently present for you emotionally? Were they attuned to your needs, or were you left to navigate your emotions on your own? If love and care were given inconsistently, you likely internalized a sense of unpredictability around relationships. When a child doesn't know if their emotional needs will be met, they develop strategies to cope. These strategies often look like emotional withdrawal or hypervigilance, constantly scanning the environment for signs that things might go wrong.

As a child, these strategies served a purpose. They protected you from disappointment or emotional pain. But as an adult, these same strategies can hinder you from forming the deep, meaningful relationships you crave. The fear of being hurt, of being abandoned, becomes so overwhelming that you start to avoid intimacy altogether. You might long for connection, but the fear of getting too close feels too risky. So, you pull away, even when what you want most is to be held closer.

This is the paradox of avoidance: the very thing you long for is the thing you are most afraid of. And that fear doesn't come from nowhere; it has its roots in those early experiences where love may have felt uncertain or even unsafe.

How Fear of Rejection and Intimacy Develops

When love and care feel unpredictable, it's only natural for fear to grow. As children, we learn to associate closeness with both comfort and potential pain. If your caregivers were sometimes loving and sometimes distant, you may have developed a belief that love is something that can be taken away at any moment. And with that belief comes a deep fear of rejection.

The fear of rejection often stems from feeling emotionally abandoned during those critical early years. Even if your caregivers were physically present, emotional absence can be just as impactful. You may have felt like your emotions were too much for them to handle, or that expressing your needs made you vulnerable to being ignored or dismissed. Over time, this creates a belief that your emotions are dangerous, that letting someone see the real you will only lead to rejection.

Intimacy, then, becomes something to fear. Letting someone in means exposing yourself to the possibility of being hurt, just as you may have been hurt in the past. This fear becomes so ingrained that it feels safer to keep people at a distance, to avoid vulnerability at all costs.

The thing about fearful avoidant attachment is that the fear of rejection is not just theoreticalit feels very real. It's not just about fearing the possibility of being left; it's about believing that if someone gets too close, they will eventually see something in you that makes them pull away. It's the belief that your needs, your emotions, or your very self is somehow "too much" for others to handle.

This belief, while deeply rooted, is not the truth. It's a story you've been telling yourself for years, shaped by the inconsistencies in love and care you experienced as a child. And while that story may have served to protect you in the past, it no longer serves you now.

Healing begins when you start to challenge that story, when you begin to see that intimacy doesn't have to equal rejection, and that being vulnerable doesn't make you weak or unlovable. It makes you human.

Guided Meditation to Explore Childhood Patterns

One of the most powerful ways to begin healing from the roots of avoidance is to bring gentle awareness to the childhood patterns that shaped you. This guided meditation will help you explore those early experiences with compassion and curiosity, allowing you to reconnect with the child you once were and begin the process of healing those old wounds.

- **Step 1: Find a quiet space**

Settle into a comfortable position in a quiet space where you won't be disturbed. Close your eyes and take a few deep breaths, allowing yourself to relax. Feel your body supported by the surface beneath you, and let go of any tension in your muscles.

- **Step 2: Connect with your breath**

Bring your attention to your breath. Notice the rise and fall of your chest as you inhale and exhale. Allow your breath to be slow and steady, creating a sense of calm within you. With each exhale, let go of any thoughts or distractions, and with each inhale, invite a sense of peace and openness.

- **Step 3: Visualize your younger self**

Now, in your mind's eye, picture yourself as a child. This could be at any age that feels significant to you, perhaps a time when you felt vulnerable or unsure. See yourself clearly in this moment. Notice what you looked like, what you were wearing, and the expression on your face.

- **Step 4: Observe your emotions**

As you focus on this younger version of yourself, gently observe the emotions that arise. What was this child feeling at that moment? Were they longing for love or comfort? Were they feeling afraid or uncertain? Allow yourself to simply observe without judgment, knowing that whatever emotions arise are valid.

- **Step 5: Offer compassion to your younger self**

Now, imagine that you, as your adult self, are standing next to this child. You are here to offer comfort and compassion. In your mind, tell this younger version of yourself that they are safe, that they are loved, and that it's okay to feel what they are feeling. Offer them the reassurance that they may not have received in the past. Let them know that you are here for them, and that they don't have to carry these burdens alone anymore.

- **Step 6: Releasing the fear**

As you continue to comfort your younger self, imagine that the fear they've been carrying is slowly being lifted. With each breath, see the fear dissolve, replaced by a sense of peace and safety. Tell this child that it's okay to let go of the fear, that they are worthy of love and connection, and that they don't need to protect themselves from rejection anymore.

- **Step 7: Return to the present moment**

When you're ready, gently bring your attention back to the present moment. Feel the surface beneath you again, notice your breath, and slowly open your eyes. Take a moment to reflect on the experience. How did it feel to connect with your younger self? What emotions came up for you during the meditation?

This meditation is a way of reconnecting with the parts of yourself that have been shaped by fear. By offering compassion to your younger self, you begin to heal the wounds that have kept you in a state of avoidance. It's a practice that you can return to whenever you feel overwhelmed by fear or when you notice old patterns of avoidance starting to surface.

As you move forward, remember that healing is not about erasing the past,it's about understanding it, and choosing to respond to it with compassion. The roots of your avoidance run deep, but they do not define who you are. You are capable of love, of intimacy, and of deep connection. And as you continue to explore and heal these early patterns, you will find that the fear that once held you back begins to loosen its grip.

Your past may have shaped you, but it doesn't have to control you. You have the power to rewrite the story of your relationships, one rooted in trust, connection, and the belief that you are worthy of love just as you are.

CHAPTER 4

How Fear Sabotages Relationships

Fear is a powerful force. When it comes to relationships, fear can quietly weave itself into the fabric of how we interact, how we love, and how we trust. The fear of being hurt, rejected, or abandoned can lead to behaviors that sabotage even the most promising relationships. Many times, we aren't fully aware of how fear operates beneath the surface, subtly influencing our actions in ways that push love away. But fear's influence is there, and it can turn our desire for connection into a source of anxiety and self-doubt.

Recognizing how fear sabotages relationships is essential if you want to break the cycle. Fear doesn't always show up as obvious panic or withdrawal. Often, it disguises itself as self-sabotage, manifesting through behaviors that seem justified or rational in the moment but ultimately create distance and erode intimacy. To understand how fear operates, we must first look at how it plays out in your romantic life, often sabotaging relationships before they even have a chance to thrive.

Recognizing Self-Sabotage in Your Romantic Life

Self-sabotage can be incredibly subtle, and it often hides behind actions that seem to have good intentions. The trouble is that these actions are rooted in fear rather than love. You might want intimacy and connection, but fear has taught you to protect yourself at all costs. And so, you build walls around your heart, convincing yourself that keeping people at a distance will keep you safe.

But what does self-sabotage actually look like in a relationship? It isn't always about dramatic fights or pushing someone away in obvious ways. Sometimes, it's the little things that add up over time,the small ways you withdraw or create distance because vulnerability feels too dangerous.

For instance, have you ever found yourself starting an argument over something trivial, just when things were going well with your partner? Maybe you criticized something insignificant, or perhaps you grew distant after a particularly close moment. This is one of the most common forms of self-sabotage,creating conflict as a way to disrupt intimacy. It's as though part of you believes that if you get too close, it will only hurt more when things inevitably fall apart.

Another classic form of self-sabotage is emotional withdrawal. You might notice that after moments of vulnerability, when you've let your guard down and shared something deeply personal, you feel the urge to pull back. Maybe you become distant or less affectionate, or perhaps you convince yourself that you need "space." This emotional retreat is fear's way of protecting you from the perceived risk of intimacy. You want to be close, but you're scared of what might happen if you fully let someone in.

Overanalyzing your partner's behavior is another way fear creeps into your relationships. You might find yourself constantly questioning their motives, even when they've given you no reason to doubt their intentions. Maybe you replay conversations in your head, looking for hidden meanings or signs that they don't really care about you. This kind of thinking doesn't just create anxiety,it erodes trust, making it difficult for your relationship to grow.

Fear can also cause you to reject love before it even has a chance to take root. Perhaps you've ended relationships prematurely, not because things were going poorly, but because the idea of being vulnerable for an extended period felt too risky. This is a form of self-protection,cutting things off before you have a chance to get hurt. But in doing so, you also prevent yourself from experiencing the deep, lasting love you truly want.

The irony of self-sabotage is that it leads to the very outcome you fear most. You push people away to protect yourself from rejection or abandonment, but in doing so, you create the very disconnection you're trying to avoid. This is the painful paradox of fearful avoidant attachment: you crave love and closeness, but your fear of vulnerability keeps you from fully embracing it.

Understanding the Roots of Self-Sabotage

To break free from the cycle of self-sabotage, it's important to understand where it comes from. These behaviors are not random; they are deeply rooted in past experiences, often going back to childhood. If you grew up in an environment where love was inconsistent or conditional, you might have learned early on that closeness comes with a cost. Maybe love was given and then taken away, or perhaps you experienced emotional abandonment from the people who were supposed to protect and nurture you.

As a child, you likely developed ways to protect yourself from the pain of rejection or abandonment. Maybe you withdraw emotionally, or perhaps you learned to anticipate rejection and cut ties before it could happen. These coping mechanisms might have helped you survive emotionally when you were younger, but as an adult, they no longer serve you. Instead, they keep you stuck in a cycle of fear and disconnection.

At the core of self-sabotage is the fear of vulnerability. Letting someone see the real you the parts of you that you hide away out of fear of judgment or rejection, feels like the ultimate risk. But here's the truth: without vulnerability, there can be no real connection. Love requires you to show up fully, flaws and all, and trust that you are enough.

It's natural to be afraid of getting hurt. After all, love does come with risks. But self-sabotage doesn't protect you from pain; it simply prevents you from experiencing the joy and fulfillment that come with deep, meaningful relationships. The fear of vulnerability might feel like it's protecting you, but in reality, it's keeping you isolated.

Relationship Mapping to Understand Behavior Patterns

One of the most effective ways to break the cycle of self-sabotage is to become aware of the patterns that have been playing out in your romantic life. Relationship mapping is a powerful tool that allows you to see these patterns more clearly, giving you insight into how fear has influenced your behavior and how you can begin to change.

Step 1: Choose a past or current relationship

To start, pick a relationship that has been significant in your life. This could be a current romantic relationship, a past relationship, or even a close friendship where similar patterns of avoidance or sabotage have shown up. The goal is to choose a relationship where you've noticed recurring behaviors or emotions tied to fear and avoidance.

Step 2: Create a timeline of key moments

On a blank sheet of paper, draw a timeline of the relationship. Mark down significant events or turning points, especially moments where you noticed yourself pulling away, starting conflicts, or feeling anxious about closeness. These moments could be as simple as the first time you felt the need for space, or more intense, like a time when you ended the relationship out of fear.

For example:

- *The first time you felt scared after your partner expressed their love.*
- *A time when you avoided a deep conversation because it felt too vulnerable.*

- *A moment when you started a fight or withdrew emotionally, even though things were going well.*

Step 3: Identify recurring behaviors

Once you've mapped out the key moments, take a step back and look for patterns. Do you notice a cycle of pushing people away after moments of closeness? Are there specific triggers, like discussions about the future, that make you feel anxious and lead to distancing behaviors? Pay attention to any recurring actions or thoughts that seem tied to fear or insecurity.

For example, you might notice that every time you and your partner had a serious conversation about commitment, you began to feel overwhelmed and started picking fights. Or you might see that after moments of vulnerability, you often withdrew emotionally, feeling the need to protect yourself from potential hurt.

Step 4: Reflect on the role of fear

Now that you've identified your patterns, reflect on the role that fear has played in these behaviors. Ask yourself:

- *What was I afraid of in these moments? Was it rejection, abandonment, or getting too close?*

- *How did my fear influence my actions? Did I push my partner away, withdraw emotionally, or sabotage the relationship in some way?*
- *What would have happened if I had chosen to lean into the relationship instead of pulling away? What if I had faced my fear instead of letting it control me?*

Write down your reflections. This step is about gaining clarity, not judgment. The goal is to understand how fear has been influencing your relationships so that you can begin to make different choices.

Step 5: Imagine a different path

Now that you have a clearer understanding of how self-sabotage has played out in your relationships, it's time to imagine what your relationship would look like if fear weren't in control. What if, instead of withdrawing after moments of closeness, you allowed yourself to stay open and vulnerable? What if, instead of assuming the worst, you chose to trust your partner's intentions?

Write down this new story. It might feel unfamiliar at first, but that's okay. Change always feels a little uncomfortable in the beginning. The important thing is that you're starting to imagine a new way of being one where love and trust take the lead, rather than fear.

Self-sabotage can feel like an invisible force that keeps you from experiencing the love you long for, but once you start to recognize it, you can begin to dismantle it. You have the power to change these patterns, to choose vulnerability over fear, and to allow yourself to experience the deep, meaningful relationships you deserve.

Healing from fearful avoidant attachment is a journey, and it won't happen all at once. But with each small step you take each time you choose trust over self-protection you move closer to the kind of love and connection that can truly transform your life. The first step is recognizing that fear doesn't have to run the show anymore. You do.

CHAPTER 5

The Inner Child and Attachment Trauma

Deep inside all of us, no matter how old we are, there exists a part of us that remains untouched by time, our inner child. This part of you carries the earliest experiences of love, safety, and connection. But it also carries the wounds. When these early experiences are shaped by inconsistency, neglect, or trauma, the inner child becomes the keeper of pain that lingers far into adulthood.

For many people with fearful avoidant attachment, it is the inner child who holds the weight of past fears and unmet needs. The fear of intimacy, the drive to protect yourself from being hurt, and the emotional push and pull in relationships are often born from the pain your inner child endured. This chapter is about reconnecting with that part of yourself, not to relive the pain, but to begin the process of healing it.

When we talk about attachment trauma, we're talking about the experiences that disrupted your ability to feel safe in relationships. It may have been a parent who was physically present but emotionally unavailable. Or it could have been a caregiver who showed love inconsistently, leaving you uncertain of when you could count on them. These early wounds don't just fade with time,they shape how you relate to yourself and others, often creating a sense of mistrust and fear in relationships.

Reconnecting with your inner child is one of the most powerful steps you can take toward healing from attachment trauma. This part of you still carries the beliefs and emotions that were formed during those early years, and until you address them, they will continue to influence your relationships in ways you may not fully understand. But here's the beautiful truth: the child within you is not broken. They are simply waiting for the love, care, and attention they didn't receive in the past. And now, as an adult, you have the power to give that to them.

Reconnecting with the Part of You That Needs Healing

Many of us go through life without ever acknowledging our inner child. We push down the pain, ignore the fear, and convince ourselves that we've moved on from the past. But no matter how much time passes, the wounds of the inner child don't disappear on their own. They show up in your adult life, often in ways you don't expect.

Maybe you notice that certain situations trigger an overwhelming emotional response that seems disproportionate to the moment. Or perhaps you find yourself reacting defensively in relationships, even when you logically know that your partner isn't trying to hurt you. These reactions are often rooted in the unresolved pain of the inner child, the part of you that learned long ago that love and safety are uncertain.

The first step in healing this part of yourself is simply acknowledging that your inner child exists. This might sound strange at first after all, you're an adult, living an adult life. But your inner child is not about your age. It's about the emotional part of you that was shaped by your earliest experiences. That part of you is still there, still holding onto the beliefs and feelings that were formed during those formative years.

When you reconnect with your inner child, you begin to see that many of your fears and insecurities are not a reflection of who you are today they are echoes from the past. The fear of being abandoned, the mistrust of love, the need to protect yourself from emotional pain,these are all responses that your inner child learned in order to survive. And while those responses may have been necessary at one time, they are no longer serving you in the present.

Healing begins when you give your inner child what they didn't receive all those years ago: love, compassion, and reassurance. It's about showing that part of yourself that they are safe now, that they don't have to keep carrying the burden of fear and pain. You are here now, as an adult, and you can protect and care for them in a way that no one else did.

Visualization to Heal Your Inner Child

One of the most effective ways to reconnect with and heal your inner child is through visualization. This exercise is designed to help you gently explore the parts of yourself that are still holding onto attachment trauma, offering them the care and compassion they need to heal.

- **Step 1: Find a quiet, comfortable space**

Begin by finding a quiet space where you won't be interrupted. Sit or lie down in a comfortable position, and take a few deep breaths. Allow yourself to relax, letting go of any tension in your body.

- **Step 2: Focus on your breath**

Close your eyes and bring your attention to your breath. Inhale slowly and deeply, filling your lungs with air, and then exhale gently, releasing any stress or anxiety. With each breath, allow yourself to become more grounded in the present moment. Feel the weight of your body supported by the surface beneath you, and let your mind begin to quiet.

- **Step 3: Visualize your inner child**

Now, in your mind's eye, picture yourself as a child. You can choose any age that feels significant whether it's a time when you felt vulnerable, hurt, or unsure. See yourself clearly as this child, noticing the details of how you looked, what you were wearing, and the expression on your face. This is the part of you that has been carrying the weight of your early experiences.

Take a moment to observe how this child feels. Are they sad, scared, or anxious? Or perhaps they feel a sense of loneliness or uncertainty. Whatever emotions come up, simply acknowledge them without judgment. This is your inner child's reality, shaped by the experiences they lived through.

- **Step 4: Offer comfort and reassurance**

Now, imagine that you, as your adult self, are standing next to this child. You are here to offer comfort, love, and reassurance. Kneel down to their level, making eye contact, and gently tell them that you see their pain, that you understand what they went through. Let them know that they are safe now, that you are here to protect them, and that they no longer have to carry these burdens alone.

If it feels right, you can reach out and hold their hand or give them a hug. Offer them the warmth and care they may not have received when they needed it most. In this moment, you are giving your inner child what they've been waiting for all along: love without conditions.

- **Step 5: Releasing old fears**

As you continue to comfort your inner child, imagine that the fear, pain, and confusion they've been holding onto begin to dissolve. With each breath, see those heavy emotions lifting away, replaced by a sense of peace and safety. Tell your inner child that they are enough, just as they are. They don't need to be afraid of rejection or abandonment anymore, because you are here to stay.

You can visualize a warm light surrounding the two of you, symbolizing love and protection. This light grows brighter and more comforting with each passing moment, filling both you and your inner child with a deep sense of calm and security.

- **Step 6: Return to the present**

When you're ready, gently bring your attention back to the present moment. Feel the surface beneath you again, notice the rhythm of your breath, and slowly open your eyes. Take a moment to reflect on the experience. How did it feel to connect with your inner child? What emotions came up for you during the visualization?

You can repeat this visualization as often as you like, especially in moments when you feel triggered or when old fears resurface. Each time you connect with your inner child, you are strengthening the bond between the past and the present, allowing healing to take place in a way that brings lasting peace.

Healing your inner child is not something that happens overnight. It's a process of reconnecting with the parts of yourself that have been buried under layers of fear and protection. But with each step you take, you move closer to a place of wholeness, a place where your past no longer dictates your present.

The more you nurture and care for your inner child, the more you will begin to notice shifts in how you relate to yourself and others. The fear that once kept you distant and guarded will start to loosen its grip, replaced by a sense of trust and openness. You will begin to see that the love you've been seeking is not something you have to chase after,it's something you can create within yourself.

This journey of healing is about coming home to yourself, to the child within you who has always been deserving of love and safety. And as you continue to heal, you will find that the relationships you create will no longer be based on fear or insecurity. Instead, they will be grounded in the knowledge that you are worthy of love, just as you are.

Your inner child has been waiting for you to show up. Now is the time to offer them the love and care they've always deserved. As you do, you will discover that healing the past is the key to creating a future filled with connection, trust, and emotional freedom.

CHAPTER 6

Overcoming the Fear of Vulnerability

Vulnerability is at the heart of every deep connection we form, yet for many, the idea of being truly vulnerable feels dangerous. It is no wonder that so many of us shy away from it, choosing instead to build walls around ourselves in an effort to feel safe. But those same walls that protect you from potential harm also block you from experiencing the closeness and intimacy you long for. This chapter is about understanding why vulnerability feels so risky and learning how to open up without fear, one small step at a time.

If you've spent much of your life in protective mode guarding your heart, avoiding situations that feel too emotionally exposed then it's no surprise that vulnerability feels foreign, maybe even impossible. But here's the truth: vulnerability is not about weakness. It's about strength, about being brave enough to show up fully, even when you can't predict the outcome. And while it may feel terrifying at first, vulnerability is the gateway to the kinds of relationships that offer real connection and fulfillment.

Why Vulnerability Feels Dangerous

At its core, the fear of vulnerability stems from a deep-rooted belief that if people see the real you,your flaws, your fears, your insecurities,they won't love you anymore. For someone with a fearful avoidant attachment style, this fear often runs deep, shaped by past experiences where being open or trusting led to hurt, rejection, or betrayal.

When you've learned to associate closeness with potential pain, it makes perfect sense that you would avoid vulnerability. You might have been conditioned, early on, to believe that letting your guard down would only invite disappointment. Maybe you were emotionally open with someone in the past, only to be dismissed or ignored. Or perhaps you learned that showing your true feelings made you more likely to be hurt or taken advantage of. Whatever the reason, these experiences left a mark, teaching you that vulnerability was dangerous.

But here's the thing: vulnerability isn't inherently dangerous. What makes it feel that way is the stories we've been told about it, or the painful experiences we've had when we were younger. Vulnerability can be incredibly scary because it requires you to let go of control. And for someone who's been protecting themselves for so long, that can feel like stepping into the unknown.

Yet, without vulnerability, real connection is impossible. When you hide behind walls of protection, the people who love you can't fully reach you. You may feel safe, but you'll also feel disconnected. Vulnerability, while risky, is the key to unlocking deeper, more meaningful relationships. It's the foundation for trust, intimacy, and emotional closeness.

Steps to Open Up Without Fear

Opening up can feel overwhelming, especially if you've spent years guarding yourself. But vulnerability doesn't have to be an all-or-nothing endeavor. You don't have to dive headfirst into deep emotional conversations or share your innermost fears all at once. Instead, think of vulnerability as something you can build slowly, one small step at a time.

Here are some steps you can take to begin practicing vulnerability in a way that feels safe and manageable:

1. Start Small
You don't need to share your deepest secrets right away. Start by practicing vulnerability in smaller, everyday moments. This could be as simple as expressing your true feelings when someone asks how you're doing, or

sharing a personal thought or experience with a trusted friend. The key is to allow yourself to be open, even in small ways, without the need to immediately retreat.

For example, if someone asks how your day went, instead of defaulting to a simple "fine," you might share something more honest, like, "It was actually a bit stressful, but I'm handling it." These small acts of openness build your tolerance for vulnerability over time.

2. Notice Your Triggers

Pay attention to the moments when you feel the urge to close off or withdraw. These are usually moments when vulnerability feels too risky. Perhaps you're in a conversation that starts to get a little too deep, or someone is offering you more emotional support than you're comfortable with. When you feel yourself pulling back, take a moment to pause and reflect on what's triggering that reaction.

Understanding your triggers is a crucial step in breaking the cycle of avoidance. Once you recognize what situations make you feel vulnerable, you can begin to challenge the belief that those moments are dangerous.

3. Practice in Safe Spaces

Vulnerability doesn't mean opening up to everyone. It's important to practice being vulnerable with people who have shown themselves to be trustworthy. These are individuals who support you, respect your boundaries, and have proven over time that they won't judge or reject you for being open.

Start by sharing something small with a trusted friend or family member. Notice how they respond. Chances are, their reaction will be one of empathy, understanding, or support. The more you practice vulnerability in safe spaces, the more you'll begin to realize that being open doesn't automatically lead to hurt.

4. Allow Imperfection
Part of the fear of vulnerability comes from the belief that we need to be perfect to be loved. But the truth is, no one is perfect, and the people who truly love you don't expect you to be. Vulnerability is about showing up as your imperfect self, with all your flaws, fears, and insecurities.

Give yourself permission to be human. When you feel the need to hide your imperfections, remind yourself that it's okay to be seen as you are. In fact, it's often our imperfections that make us relatable and loveable. Letting others see the real you creates deeper connections and allows people to love you for who you truly are.

5. Lean Into Discomfort

Vulnerability will likely feel uncomfortable at first, especially if you've spent a long time avoiding it. That discomfort doesn't mean you're doing something wrong,it's a sign that you're growing. When you feel the discomfort of vulnerability, lean into it instead of running away. Acknowledge the fear, but don't let it dictate your actions.

Over time, the discomfort will lessen as you become more accustomed to being open. Vulnerability may never feel completely comfortable, but it will start to feel more natural as you practice.

Safe Vulnerability Practice with Trusted Individuals

This exercise is designed to help you practice vulnerability in a safe and supportive environment. The goal is to slowly build your tolerance for being open, allowing you to experience the benefits of vulnerability without overwhelming yourself.

Step 1: Choose a Trusted Person

Identify someone in your life who you feel safe with,someone who has shown themselves to be kind, supportive, and trustworthy. This could be a close friend, a family member, or a partner. The important thing is that this person has proven, over time, that they respect your boundaries and care about your well-being.

Step 2: Set an Intention

Before you engage in a vulnerable conversation, take a moment to set an intention. What do you want to share? Why is it important to you? Your intention might be something simple, like, "I want to practice being more open about my feelings," or "I want to share something personal that I've been holding back."

Setting an intention helps ground you in the moment and gives you a sense of purpose as you practice vulnerability.

Step 3: Share Something Small

Start by sharing something small with the person you've chosen. It doesn't have to be anything major, just a personal thought or feeling that you wouldn't normally share. For example, you might say, "I've been feeling a bit anxious lately," or "I've been thinking a lot about how hard it is for me to ask for help when I need it."

As you share, pay attention to how the other person responds. Do they offer support, empathy, or validation? Notice how it feels to be seen and heard, and remind yourself that it's okay to be open in these moments.

Step 4: Reflect on the Experience

After the conversation, take some time to reflect on how it felt to be vulnerable. Was it more or less difficult than you expected? How did the other person respond? How did you feel afterward? Write down your thoughts and feelings in a journal, noting any insights or observations about the experience.

This reflection is an important part of the process, as it allows you to see how vulnerability affects you emotionally. Over time, these reflections will help you build a deeper understanding of your relationship with vulnerability and how you can continue to practice it in healthy ways.

Note:

Vulnerability is one of the greatest gifts you can give to yourself and others. It's the pathway to deeper connection, greater intimacy, and true emotional freedom. Yes, it's scary. Yes, it feels risky. But the rewards are worth the discomfort. When you allow yourself to be seen, just as you are, you open the door to a kind of love and connection that isn't possible behind walls of self-protection.

Each step you take toward vulnerability brings you closer to the relationships you've always wanted, relationships built on trust, honesty, and mutual support. And as you continue to practice, you'll begin to realize that vulnerability isn't about being weak or exposed. It's about being strong enough to show up fully, even when you're afraid.

> *The fear of vulnerability may never completely go away, but with practice, you'll learn to carry it with you as you step into deeper, more fulfilling relationships.*

CHAPTER 7

Emotional Regulation and Stability

Emotions can feel like an unstoppable force, rushing through us without warning, often leaving us overwhelmed and unsure of how to respond. Whether it's the rising wave of anxiety, the sudden sting of anger, or the sinking weight of sadness, these emotions have a way of taking over our minds and bodies. But learning to manage emotional overwhelm is one of the most transformative skills you can develop,not just for your relationships with others, but for your relationship with yourself.

When you have a fearful avoidant attachment style, emotions can feel especially intense. You may find yourself swinging between extremes,one moment craving connection, the next pushing people away in fear. Or perhaps you feel emotionally flooded, unable to process your feelings in a way that feels safe or manageable. This chapter is about finding stability in those moments when emotions seem too big to handle. It's about learning to regulate your emotions so that they no longer control you, but instead become something you can navigate with calm and clarity.

Emotional regulation doesn't mean suppressing or avoiding your feelings. In fact, the opposite is true. It's about understanding your emotions, acknowledging them, and finding healthy ways to respond. When you learn to regulate your emotions, you create a sense of inner stability,a groundedness that allows you to move through life's ups and downs without being swept away.

<u>Tools for Managing Emotional Overwhelm</u>

There are many ways to manage emotional overwhelm, and what works best for you will depend on your personal needs and experiences. The key is to develop a toolkit of strategies that you can turn to when you start to feel overwhelmed. These tools won't make your emotions disappear, but they will help you stay grounded and prevent your feelings from spiraling out of control.

Here are some powerful tools for managing emotional overwhelm:

1. Name Your Emotions

One of the most effective ways to regulate emotions is to simply name what you're feeling. It sounds almost too simple to be true, but research shows that labeling your emotions helps to reduce their intensity. When you're in the midst of an emotional storm, take a moment to pause and ask yourself, "What am I feeling right now?" Are you anxious, angry, sad, or frustrated? By naming the emotion, you're bringing awareness to it, which can help you feel more in control.

For example, if you're feeling overwhelmed by anxiety, saying to yourself, "I'm feeling anxious right now," can help you separate the emotion from your sense of self. It's not that *you* are anxious; it's that you're *experiencing* anxiety. This small shift in perspective can create space between you and the emotion, making it feel less all-consuming.

2. Ground Yourself in the Present Moment

Emotions often pull us out of the present and into a cycle of worry about the future or regret about the past. Grounding techniques are designed to bring you back to the present moment, helping you break free from that cycle. One simple way to ground yourself is through mindfulness practices that focus on your senses.

For example, try the "5-4-3-2-1" technique:

- Look around and name **five** things you can see.
- Touch **four** things around you (e.g., the texture of your clothing, the feel of your chair).
- Listen for **three** different sounds.
- Identify **two** things you can smell.
- Acknowledge **one** thing you can taste.

This exercise redirects your attention away from your swirling emotions and into the tangible world around you. It brings you back to the present moment, where you have more control over your response to what you're feeling.

3. Practice Self-Compassion

When you're feeling overwhelmed, it's easy to fall into self-criticism. You might tell yourself that you "shouldn't" be feeling this way or that you're overreacting. But this kind of thinking only adds more emotional weight to what you're already experiencing. Instead, try practicing self-compassion.

Self-compassion means treating yourself with the same kindness and understanding that you would offer to a friend who's struggling. When your emotions feel too big, remind yourself that it's okay to feel what you're feeling. Emotions are a natural part of being human, and they don't make you weak or broken. In fact, by offering yourself compassion, you create a space for healing and growth.

Try saying to yourself: "This is a tough moment, but I'm doing the best I can. It's okay to feel this way, and I will get through it."

4. Use Visualization Techniques

Visualization can be a powerful tool for emotional regulation. When emotions feel overwhelming, it can help to visualize a calming or peaceful scene in your mind. This could be a place where you feel safe and relaxed, such as a beach, a forest, or even a cozy room in your home.

Close your eyes and imagine yourself in this place. Picture all the details,the sights, sounds, smells, and sensations. Imagine the feel of the sun on your skin, the sound of the waves, or the warmth of the fire. As you immerse yourself in this visualization, notice how your body and mind begin to relax. Visualization helps create distance between you and your emotions, allowing you to return to a place of calm.

5. Set Boundaries Around Emotional Triggers

If certain situations or people tend to trigger emotional overwhelm, it's important to set boundaries to protect your emotional well-being. Boundaries can take many forms, from limiting contact with individuals who drain your energy to giving yourself permission to step away from emotionally charged conversations.

Setting boundaries is an act of self-care. It's not about avoiding difficult emotions entirely, but rather about managing your emotional energy in a way that allows you to stay balanced and grounded. If you know that a certain situation will leave you feeling emotionally drained, take steps to protect yourself by setting clear, healthy boundaries.

The 4-7-8 Breathing Technique for Calmness

When emotions start to feel overwhelming, your body often reacts by going into fight-or-flight mode. Your heart rate increases, your breathing becomes shallow, and your muscles tense up. One of the quickest ways to calm your body and mind is through conscious breathing. The 4-7-8 breathing technique is a simple yet powerful tool that can help you regulate your emotions by activating your body's relaxation response.

This breathing technique is based on ancient practices of pranayama, a form of controlled breathing used in yoga and meditation. It works by slowing down your heart rate and calming your nervous system, making it an effective way to manage emotional overwhelm in the moment.

Here's how to practice the 4-7-8 breathing technique:

Step 1: Get Comfortable
Find a quiet space where you can sit comfortably with your back straight. Rest your hands on your lap and close your eyes. Take a moment to settle into your body, releasing any tension in your shoulders, jaw, or neck.

Step 2: Inhale for 4 Seconds
Begin by inhaling slowly and deeply through your nose for a count of four. As you breathe in, focus on filling your lungs completely, expanding your belly and chest with air.

Step 3: Hold for 7 Seconds
Once you've inhaled fully, gently hold your breath for a count of seven. During this time, try to relax your body even further, allowing the breath to settle in your lungs.

Step 4: Exhale for 8 Seconds
After holding your breath, exhale slowly and steadily through your mouth for a count of eight. As you exhale, imagine that you're releasing any tension, stress, or

emotional buildup that has been weighing on you. Let the breath carry away your worries.

Step 5: Repeat
Repeat the cycle at least four times. You can continue for as long as you need, gradually extending the practice as you feel more comfortable. As you practice, you'll notice that your body begins to relax, and your mind becomes clearer.

The 4-7-8 breathing technique is a powerful tool for calming your nervous system in moments of stress or emotional overwhelm. It's especially helpful when you feel anxiety building or when you're experiencing an emotional trigger that threatens to spiral out of control.

> *Learning to regulate your emotions is not about denying or suppressing how you feel. It's about creating space between you and your emotions, so you can respond to them with wisdom rather than reacting out of fear or overwhelm. Emotional regulation helps you stay centered, even when life throws unexpected challenges your way.*

As you practice the tools outlined in this chapter, you'll begin to notice a shift in how you experience your emotions. They will still come,sometimes intensely but you'll feel more equipped to handle them. You'll trust that you can ride the waves of emotion without being pulled under.

Emotional regulation is not about becoming immune to life's difficulties. It's about developing the resilience to navigate them with grace and stability. And as you strengthen this skill, you'll find that the emotional storms that once felt overwhelming now feel more like passing clouds. You'll know that, no matter what emotions come your way, you have the tools to manage them, and that inner stability is always within reach.

CHAPTER 8

Developing Emotional Security

Emotional security is one of the most important qualities you can bring into a relationship. When you feel emotionally secure, you trust in yourself and in your ability to handle whatever challenges come your way. You don't rely on others to provide your sense of worth, and you're not constantly worried about being rejected or abandoned. Instead, you approach relationships with confidence, knowing that you can navigate both the joys and the challenges with grace.

For many people, emotional security can seem like an elusive goal, especially if past relationships have left you feeling vulnerable or unsure of yourself. But emotional security is not something you're born with; it's something you develop over time through inner strength, self-awareness, and practice. In this chapter, we'll explore how to cultivate that inner strength and bring emotional security into your relationships.

Cultivating Inner Strength in Relationships

Developing emotional security begins with cultivating inner strength. This doesn't mean putting on a tough exterior or pretending that nothing affects you. Inner strength is about building a solid foundation of self-worth and resilience, so that no matter what happens in your relationships, you remain grounded.

Here are a few key steps to building inner strength in relationships:

1. Recognize That Your Worth Comes from Within

One of the most common sources of insecurity in relationships is the belief that your worth is tied to how others see you. When you rely on external validation,whether it's from a partner, friends, or society at large,you're constantly chasing approval, which can leave you feeling anxious or unsure of yourself. To cultivate emotional security, it's essential to recognize that your worth is inherent. You don't need anyone else to validate your value. You are enough just as you are, and that truth doesn't change, regardless of what happens in your relationships.

2. Let Go of the Need for Control

Insecurity often arises from the desire to control outcomes in relationships. You might find yourself trying to predict or manage how others will respond, or worrying about what might happen in the future. But emotional security doesn't come from controlling everything around you,it comes from trusting that you can handle whatever comes your way. Letting go of control doesn't mean you stop caring; it means you trust yourself to navigate the uncertainties of life with strength and resilience.

3. Embrace Vulnerability

It might sound counterintuitive, but emotional security isn't about always being "strong" or never showing weakness. In fact, true inner strength comes from allowing yourself to be vulnerable. Vulnerability means showing up as your authentic self, even when you're afraid of being hurt. It's about being open and honest with yourself and others, knowing that you're strong enough to handle whatever the outcome may be. When you embrace vulnerability, you stop trying to protect yourself from every possible hurt, and you begin to trust in your ability to recover and grow from challenges.

4. Practice Self-Compassion

In moments of insecurity, it's easy to be hard on yourself, especially if you feel like you've made a mistake or let someone down. But emotional security requires self-compassion,the ability to treat yourself with kindness and understanding, even when things don't go as planned. Instead of criticizing yourself for not being perfect, remind yourself that you're human, and it's okay to have flaws. Self-compassion helps you build resilience by allowing you to bounce back from setbacks without losing your sense of worth.

Daily Affirmations for Emotional Resilience

Affirmations are a powerful way to shift your mindset and reinforce your inner strength. When you repeat affirmations regularly, they help to rewire your brain, replacing negative or self-doubting thoughts with more empowering beliefs. This practice can help you cultivate emotional resilience and remind you of your inherent worth.

Here's how to incorporate daily affirmations into your routine:

Step 1: Choose Affirmations That Speak to You
Start by choosing a few affirmations that resonate with you and reflect the emotional security you're working to build. Here are some examples:

- *I am worthy of love and respect, just as I am.*
- *I trust myself to navigate challenges with strength and grace.*
- *My worth is not defined by others' opinions of me.*

- *I am capable of building healthy, fulfilling relationships.*
- *I am open to vulnerability and trust in my ability to heal.*

Feel free to adapt these affirmations or create your own. The important thing is that they feel meaningful to you and align with the emotional resilience you want to cultivate.

Step 2: Make Affirmations Part of Your Daily Routine

Set aside a few minutes each day whether it's in the morning, before bed, or during a quiet moment to repeat your affirmations. You can say them out loud, write them in a journal, or even record yourself and listen to them throughout the day. Consistency is key, as the regular practice helps reinforce the positive beliefs you're trying to instill.

Step 3: Reflect on Your Progress

As you continue practicing your affirmations, take note of how they impact your mindset and emotions. Are you starting to feel more confident in yourself? Are you noticing a shift in how you approach your relationships? Journaling about your progress can help you track your growth and deepen your understanding of how affirmations are supporting your emotional resilience.

CHAPTER 9

Creating Safety in Relationships

Emotional safety is the foundation of any healthy relationship. When you feel safe with your partner, you can be your true self, express your needs, and open up about your feelings without fear of judgment or rejection. But creating that sense of safety doesn't happen by accident it requires effort, communication, and trust-building.

In this chapter, we'll explore how to build trust in your relationships without overthinking or falling into patterns of doubt. You'll learn how to create an environment where both you and your partner feel secure, and how to deepen trust through clear, honest communication.

How to Build Trust Without Overthinking

Trust is one of the most essential elements of emotional safety in a relationship. Without it, you may find yourself constantly questioning your partner's intentions or worrying about the future of the relationship. But trust doesn't come from overanalyzing every detail or trying to predict every outcome. In fact, overthinking can often undermine trust by feeding into anxiety and doubt.

Here are some key strategies for building trust in a relationship without falling into the trap of overthinking:

1. Focus on the Present, Not the Future

One of the main reasons people overthink in relationships is because they're worried about what might happen in the future. But trust is built in the present, through everyday actions and interactions. Instead of constantly trying to predict the future or worrying about what might go wrong, focus on what's happening right now. Pay attention to how your partner shows up for you in the present moment, and trust that your relationship will continue to grow based on these positive experiences.

2. Communicate Openly and Honestly

Trust is rooted in clear and honest communication. When you and your partner can talk openly about your thoughts, feelings, and concerns, it creates a foundation of transparency and mutual understanding. Instead of keeping your worries to yourself or overanalyzing situations in your head, express your feelings directly to your partner. Honest communication helps prevent misunderstandings and allows both of you to address any concerns before they grow into bigger issues.

3. Practice Self-Trust

Building trust in a relationship also requires trusting yourself. When you don't trust your own judgment, it's easy to fall into patterns of overthinking, constantly questioning whether you're making the right decisions. But when you trust yourself, you can approach your relationship with more confidence. You know that even if challenges arise, you're capable of navigating them and making choices that align with your values.

4. Let Go of Perfectionism

Many people overthink in relationships because they're afraid of making mistakes or being vulnerable. But trust isn't about perfection,it's about being willing to show up as your authentic self, even when things don't go perfectly. Letting go of perfectionism allows you to embrace the imperfections of both yourself and your partner, which in turn fosters deeper trust.

<u>Communication Exercises for Building Trust</u>

Strong communication is key to building and maintaining trust in any relationship. The following

76

exercises are designed to help you and your partner improve your communication skills and deepen your emotional connection.

Exercise 1: The "Listening Without Interrupting" Practice

One of the most common communication challenges in relationships is the tendency to interrupt or jump in with responses before the other person has finished speaking. This exercise helps both partners practice active listening without interrupting.

- *Step 1: Set aside 10-15 minutes where both you and your partner can focus on each other without distractions.*

- *Step 2: One partner starts by sharing a thought, feeling, or concern. The other partner listens without interrupting or offering advice.*

- *Step 3: Once the first partner has finished speaking, the listener can reflect back what they heard, using phrases like, "What I hear you saying is..." This helps ensure that the listener fully understands their partner's perspective.*

- *Step 4: Switch roles, allowing the other partner to share while the listener practices the same level of attention and understanding.*

This exercise helps build trust by encouraging both partners to feel heard and understood without judgment or interruption.

Exercise 2: "I Feel" Statements

Many conflicts in relationships arise because people express their feelings in ways that come across as blame or criticism. Using "I feel" statements helps you communicate your emotions without making your partner feel defensive.

- *Step 1: Choose a recent situation where you felt hurt, frustrated, or misunderstood. Identify the specific feelings you experienced in that moment.*

- *Step 2: Instead of saying, "You made me feel..." reframe your statement using "I feel" to express your emotions without placing blame on your partner. For example, you might say, "I feel anxious when plans change at the last minute," rather than, "You always change plans and it stresses me out."*

- *Step 3: Encourage your partner to respond with their feelings using the same "I feel" format. This creates a space for both partners to share without fear of escalation or defensiveness.*

- *Step 4: After both partners have shared, take a moment to reflect on what was said. Discuss any misunderstandings and clarify you*r feelings to ensure both partners feel heard and understood.

This exercise fosters a safe environment for open communication and builds trust by promoting emotional honesty and understanding.

Exercise 3: Weekly Check-Ins

Setting aside regular time to check in with each other can significantly strengthen your emotional connection and build trust. These check-ins provide an opportunity to discuss how you're feeling about the relationship and to address any concerns before they become bigger issues.

- *Step 1: Schedule a specific time each week (e.g., Sunday evenings) to sit down together and talk about your feelings regarding the relationship. Make it a routine, and treat it as a priority.*
- *Step 2: During the check-in, each partner takes turns sharing their thoughts and feelings about the week. Focus on both the positive aspects of the relationship and any areas where you feel you could improve.*
- *Step 3: Approach this conversation with an open heart, ready to listen and share without judgment. Use "I feel" statements to express your emotions and encourage your partner to do the same.*
- *Step 4: After discussing your feelings, take a few minutes to brainstorm any action steps that you both can take to strengthen your emotional connection. This might include spending more*

*quality time together, trying new acti*vities, or addressing specific concerns that have come up. Regular check-ins create a rhythm of communication that promotes trust, transparency, and emotional safety. By consistently making time for each other, you reinforce the idea that you are both committed to nurturing the relationship.

Building trust in relationships takes time and effort, but the rewards are immeasurable. As you practice these communication exercises, you'll find that trust begins to deepen, allowing for a more secure and fulfilling connection with your partner. Remember, emotional safety is a two-way street,it requires both partners to be committed to creating an environment of openness and understanding.

As you continue to develop emotional security within yourself and cultivate trust in your relationships, you'll discover that love can flourish in an atmosphere of safety, where vulnerability is welcomed, and authenticity is celebrated. You are creating a foundation that will allow your relationships to thrive, providing both you and your partner the opportunity to grow closer and build a lasting bond.

In the end, emotional security and safety are not just about avoiding pain; they are about embracing love, connection, and the beauty of being truly seen and accepted. As you embark on this journey of self-discovery and connection, remember that every step you take brings you closer to the kind of relationships you have always desired,relationships filled with trust, intimacy, and the deep joy of genuine connection.

CHAPTER 10

Rewriting Your Attachment Story

Every individual carries a unique narrative about love and connection, woven from the threads of our early experiences, relationships, and beliefs. For many with a fearful avoidant attachment style, this narrative is often shaped by fear and avoidance, leading to patterns that keep us stuck in cycles of anxiety and disconnection. But just as we have the power to tell our stories, we also have the power to rewrite them.

Rewriting your attachment story involves understanding how your past experiences have shaped your beliefs about relationships and recognizing that you can create a new narrative,one that empowers you to connect more deeply, trust more fully, and love without fear. This chapter is about taking the steps necessary to move beyond fear and avoidance, and to embrace the possibility of healthier, more fulfilling relationships.

Moving Beyond Fear and Avoidance

Fear has a way of shaping our reality, often keeping us from pursuing the connections we truly desire. It's a powerful emotion that can create barriers between us and our ability to form intimate relationships. But when you begin to rewrite your attachment story, you start to dismantle those barriers, allowing for new possibilities to emerge.

The first step in moving beyond fear is acknowledging its presence in your life. This means recognizing the ways in which fear has influenced your relationships, often causing you to pull away or avoid vulnerability. You may have experienced moments of intimacy followed by a sudden urge to retreat, or perhaps you've found yourself questioning your partner's love, even when they've shown you kindness and support.

Understanding that these fears stem from past experiences is crucial. Often, they are echoes of old wounds that have been carried into your present relationships. These fears are not a reflection of your worth or your capacity for love; they are simply remnants of the past that no longer need to define you.

Challenge Negative Beliefs

Part of rewriting your attachment story involves challenging the negative beliefs that have taken root in your mind. Perhaps you've internalized the idea that you are unlovable or that you will inevitably be hurt if you let someone in. These beliefs can feel deeply ingrained, but they are not truths; they are stories that you've been told and have come to believe.

Start by questioning these negative beliefs. Ask yourself:

- *Where did this belief come from?*
- *Is it based on facts or assumptions?*
- *What evidence do I have to support or contradict this belief?*

By examining the origins of these beliefs, you can begin to dismantle them, replacing them with more empowering narratives that reflect your true worth and potential for love.

Embrace Vulnerability

Vulnerability is a key component of forming secure attachments. While it may feel uncomfortable, embracing vulnerability allows you to connect more deeply with others. It's about taking risks, showing your true self, expressing your feelings, and being open to the possibility of connection.

As you rewrite your attachment story, practice leaning into vulnerability in small ways. Share your thoughts and feelings with trusted friends or partners. Allow yourself to be seen and heard. The more you practice vulnerability, the more you'll realize that it doesn't have to lead to pain; in fact, it often leads to deeper intimacy and connection.

Practice Self-Compassion
Moving beyond fear also requires self-compassion. Understand that changing your attachment style is a process, and it's okay to take it one step at a time. Be gentle with yourself as you navigate these changes. Recognize that you are learning and growing, and it's perfectly normal to have setbacks along the way.

Self-compassion involves treating yourself with kindness and understanding when you experience difficulties. Instead of criticizing yourself for feeling fearful or insecure, remind yourself that these feelings are valid. Everyone has fears, and it's part of being human. By practicing self-compassion, you create a safe space for growth and healing.

Writing Your New Relationship Narrative

One of the most powerful ways to rewrite your attachment story is to engage in a reflective writing exercise. This exercise allows you to articulate your experiences, challenge negative beliefs, and envision a new narrative for your relationships.

Step 1: Reflect on Your Past

Begin by taking some time to reflect on your past relationships and attachment experiences. Write down your thoughts on the following prompts:

- *What were some of the key experiences in your childhood that shaped your views on love and connection?*
- *How have those experiences influenced your attachment style and relationships as an adult?*
- *What negative beliefs do you hold about yourself or your capacity for love?*

Be honest with yourself. This reflection is about gaining clarity and understanding the roots of your attachment style.

Step 2: Identify Patterns

Next, consider the patterns you've noticed in your relationships. Write down your observations regarding how fear and avoidance have played a role in your interactions with others. Consider the following questions:

- *How have your fears of intimacy or rejection influenced your behavior in relationships?*

- *What specific situations trigger your avoidance or anxiety?*
- *Are there recurring themes in your relationships that you want to change?*

By identifying these patterns, you gain insight into how your past has shaped your present.

Step 3: Envision Your New Narrative

Now it's time to envision the narrative you want to create moving forward. Write a new relationship story for yourself,one that reflects your values, aspirations, and desires. Consider the following prompts:

- *What would a healthy, fulfilling relationship look like for you?*
- *How would you express love and vulnerability in this relationship?*
- *What beliefs would you like to adopt about yourself and your capacity for love?*

Let your imagination guide you as you paint a picture of the future you desire. Write in detail about the feelings, connections, and experiences you wish to have in your relationships.

Step 4: Affirm Your New Story

Once you have written your new narrative, it's important to affirm it regularly. Choose a few key statements from your new story and turn them into affirmations. For example:

- *"I am worthy of love and connection."*
- *"I trust myself to navigate relationships with confidence."*
- *"I embrace vulnerability as a path to deeper intimacy."*

Repeat these affirmations daily to reinforce your new narrative and help internalize the beliefs that will support your growth.

Step 5: Share Your Story
If you feel comfortable, consider sharing your new narrative with a trusted friend or partner. Sharing your story can create accountability and foster deeper connections. It also provides an opportunity for others to support you in your journey toward emotional security.

Rewriting your attachment story is a journey, and it's one that requires patience, self-reflection, and courage. As you move beyond fear and avoidance, you will find that the connections you build are richer and more fulfilling than you ever imagined possible. Your past does not have to define your future; you have the power to create a new narrative, one that celebrates your worthiness and opens the door to authentic love.

As you engage in this process, remember that you are not alone. Many others have walked this path before you, and each step you take toward healing and connection is a testament to your strength and resilience. Embrace the journey, trust the process, and allow yourself to experience the love and intimacy you deserve. Your new attachment story is waiting to be written, and it starts with the choices you make today.

CHAPTER 11

Reparenting Yourself for Emotional Growth

In the journey of healing from attachment wounds, reparenting yourself emerges as a transformative practice. This process involves stepping into the role of a compassionate caregiver for your inner child, providing the love, support, and understanding that may have been lacking in your formative years. By reparenting yourself, you create a nurturing environment within that allows for emotional growth, self-acceptance, and the development of healthier relationship patterns.

The concept of reparenting is rooted in the idea that many of the emotional struggles we face as adults can be traced back to unmet needs from childhood. If you experienced inconsistent love, emotional neglect, or trauma, you may find yourself grappling with feelings of unworthiness, fear of abandonment, or a heightened sensitivity to rejection. Reparenting offers a path to address these issues by actively meeting the needs of your inner child and rewriting the narrative of your emotional experiences.

Why Reparenting Matters for Attachment Healing

Reparenting is essential for healing because it allows you to reclaim the parts of yourself that have been hidden away due to fear and pain. It's about recognizing that the beliefs and behaviors you developed in childhood don't have to define you as an adult. Instead, you can choose to foster a sense of safety and security within yourself, which in turn influences how you engage with others.

Here are a few key reasons why reparenting is crucial for attachment healing:

1. Healing Old Wounds

When you reparent yourself, you have the opportunity to address the wounds from your past that may still be affecting your relationships today. This process involves acknowledging the pain you experienced and providing the compassion and validation that you may not have received at the time. By doing so, you begin to heal old wounds, freeing yourself from the emotional burdens they carry.

2. Cultivating Self-Compassion

Reparenting is about treating yourself with the same kindness and understanding you would offer a child. Many people with fearful avoidant attachment struggle with self-criticism and harsh judgment. Through reparenting, you learn to cultivate self-compassion, recognizing that it's okay to feel vulnerable and imperfect. This self-compassion fosters resilience and a greater sense of self-worth.

3. Establishing Emotional Safety

Creating emotional safety within yourself is a key aspect of reparenting. This involves developing a supportive inner dialogue that reassures you that you are deserving of love and care. As you nurture your inner child, you build a sense of safety that allows you to embrace vulnerability in your relationships with others.

4. Redefining Your Beliefs

Many of the limiting beliefs that hinder emotional growth are rooted in childhood experiences. Through reparenting, you can identify these beliefs and challenge their validity. Instead of holding onto beliefs that you are unworthy of love or that intimacy will always lead to pain, you can replace them with empowering truths that affirm your worthiness and capability to form healthy relationships.

Reparenting Practices for Nurturing Yourself

Engaging in reparenting practices can be incredibly healing and transformative. The following exercises will guide you in nurturing your inner child and developing a more compassionate relationship with yourself.

Step 1: Identify Your Inner Child

Begin by reflecting on your inner child. Picture yourself as a child at a specific age,perhaps at a time when you felt particularly vulnerable or in need of support. Visualize your inner child and think about their needs, fears, and desires. What did they long for? What did they struggle with? Acknowledge the emotions that arise as you connect with this part of yourself.

Step 2: Write a Letter to Your Inner Child

Take a moment to write a letter to your inner child. In this letter, express your understanding of their pain and struggles. Offer them the love and support they may not have received. Let them know that you are now here to protect and nurture them. Here's a simple structure you can follow:

- *Acknowledge Their Feelings*: *"Dear [Your Inner Child's Name], I see how sad and scared you feel when things get tough. It's okay to feel this way. You are not alone."*

- **_Offer Comfort_**: _"I want you to know that I am here for you. You are safe now, and I will take care of you."_
- **_Encourage Growth_**: _"You are brave, and you have the strength to overcome challenges. It's okay to be vulnerable and ask for help when you need it."_

Writing this letter allows you to articulate the nurturing voice that may have been absent in your childhood. It's a powerful way to affirm the emotional support your inner child deserves.

Step 3: Create a Self-Care Routine
Nurturing your inner child also means prioritizing self-care. Think about the activities that bring you joy and comfort whether it's reading a favorite book, going for a walk in nature, engaging in creative hobbies, or simply taking time to relax. Create a self-care routine that includes these activities, allowing your inner child to experience joy and safety.

Make it a point to schedule regular self-care time in your week. This can be as simple as setting aside an hour each Sunday to do something that makes you feel happy and relaxed. Remember, self-care is not a luxury; it's a necessity for your emotional well-being.

Step 4: Practice Positive Self-Talk

Throughout your day, pay attention to your inner dialogue. Notice if you tend to be critical or harsh on yourself, especially when you make mistakes or feel insecure. Begin practicing positive self-talk by consciously choosing to replace negative thoughts with affirming statements.

For example:

- *Instead of saying, "I can't believe I messed that up," try saying, "It's okay to make mistakes; I'm learning and growing."*
- *Replace "I'm not good enough" with "I am worthy of love and acceptance just as I am."*

This practice helps rewire your thinking patterns and reinforces the nurturing messages you are giving to your inner child.

Step 5: Engage in Playfulness

Remember the joy of play from your childhood? Engaging in playful activities can be a wonderful way to reconnect with your inner child. This could be anything from drawing, dancing, playing games, or even just being silly. Allow yourself to embrace moments of joy and laughter, free from judgment or self-consciousness.

Set aside time each week for play, whether it's with friends, family, or just by yourself. Embracing playfulness invites a sense of lightness into your life, reminding you that it's okay to have fun and enjoy the present moment.

Reparenting yourself is a journey that requires patience and dedication. It's about reclaiming the parts of yourself that may have felt lost or neglected, and offering them the love and nurturing they deserve. As you engage in these practices, you will find that emotional growth becomes not only possible but also deeply rewarding.

By nurturing your inner child and developing a compassionate relationship with yourself, you create a foundation for lasting change. Emotional security blossoms from this place of self-acceptance and care, allowing you to engage with the world and your relationships in a healthier, more fulfilling way.

As you continue this journey of reparenting, remember that healing is not a linear process. There will be ups and downs, and that's perfectly normal. Be gentle with yourself as you navigate this path, and trust that you are capable of rewriting your attachment story into one that reflects your strength, resilience, and deep capacity for love.

CHAPTER 12

Understanding Emotional Boundaries

In the landscape of relationships, emotional boundaries serve as the vital lines that protect our well-being and foster healthy connections with others. They define where we end and others begin, allowing us to establish a sense of self while engaging with the people we care about. Understanding and setting emotional boundaries is crucial, especially for those of us navigating the complexities of fearful avoidant attachment. It enables us to cultivate connections that are both meaningful and respectful, without compromising our emotional safety.

For many, the idea of setting boundaries can evoke anxiety. You might fear that creating distance will push people away or that it will lead to conflict. However, boundaries are not about building walls; they are about defining limits that create space for love, respect, and understanding. Establishing clear emotional boundaries helps you articulate your needs while honoring the needs of others. This chapter will explore the importance of emotional boundaries and how to set them in a way that promotes healthy relationships.

Setting Boundaries Without Pushing People Away

The key to setting effective emotional boundaries is understanding that they are necessary for both your well-being and the well-being of your relationships. Boundaries are not about shutting others out; rather, they are about allowing healthy interactions to flourish. Here are several principles to keep in mind as you navigate this process:

1. Recognize Your Needs

Before you can set boundaries, you must first understand what your needs are. What makes you feel safe and respected in a relationship? What triggers feelings of discomfort or overwhelm? Spend some time reflecting on your emotional landscape. Are there certain topics that you find difficult to discuss? Are there behaviors that consistently leave you feeling drained or anxious?

Identifying your needs is the first step in establishing boundaries. When you are clear about what you require for your emotional well-being, you can communicate those needs more effectively.

2. Communicate Clearly and Compassionately

Setting boundaries is often about effective communication. It's important to express your needs in a way that is clear, respectful, and compassionate. Avoid vague language or passive-aggressive comments. Instead, use "I" statements that focus on your feelings and needs. For example, instead of saying, "You always interrupt me," try, "I feel unheard when I'm interrupted. I would appreciate it if we could each take turns speaking."

Communicating your boundaries clearly allows others to understand your perspective and respect your needs. This approach fosters open dialogue and reduces the likelihood of misunderstanding or conflict.

3. Be Firm Yet Kind

When setting boundaries, it's important to be firm about your needs while also maintaining a tone of kindness. Boundaries can sometimes be met with resistance, especially if the other person is used to a different dynamic. Remind yourself that it's okay to stand firm in your boundaries, even if it feels uncomfortable. You are advocating for your emotional well-being, and that is a valid and necessary act.

When you communicate your boundaries, do so with a calm and kind demeanor. You might say, "I value our relationship, and for us to maintain a positive connection, I need to set a boundary around this topic."

4. Expect Resistance but Stay Committed

It's natural to encounter some resistance when

establishing boundaries. People may not fully understand why you are setting them or may feel challenged by your new expectations. Be prepared for pushback, and remind yourself that this is a part of the process. It doesn't mean that your boundaries are wrong; it simply means you are adjusting the dynamics of the relationship.

Stay committed to your boundaries and be patient as others adjust. Over time, those who respect you will come to understand and honor your limits, leading to healthier and more satisfying relationships.

5. Practice Self-Reflection
After setting a boundary, take time to reflect on how it felt. Did you feel empowered? Anxious? Resentful? This self-reflection can provide valuable insights into your emotional landscape and help you understand how boundaries impact your well-being. If you feel good about the boundary you set, celebrate that success! If you notice lingering discomfort or regret, explore those feelings to determine if the boundary needs adjusting or if additional boundaries should be considered.

Boundary-Setting Scenarios and Scripts

The following exercise will help you practice setting boundaries in various scenarios. By role-playing these situations and developing scripts, you can gain confidence in your ability to communicate your needs effectively.

Step 1: Identify Common Boundary Scenarios

Start by identifying specific situations where you feel your boundaries are often crossed or where you struggle to communicate your needs. Here are a few examples to consider:

- *A friend frequently cancels plans at the last minute, leaving you feeling unimportant.*
- *A family member often makes critical comments about your choices, leading to feelings of inadequacy.*
- *A partner frequently interrupts you during conversations, causing frustration.*

Step 2: Write Scripts for Each Scenario

For each scenario, write a script that outlines how you would communicate your boundary. Use "I" statements to express your feelings and needs clearly. Here are examples based on the scenarios mentioned:

Scenario 1: Friend Cancels Plans

Script: "I really value our time together, and when plans get canceled at the last minute, I feel disappointed and unimportant. I would appreciate it if we could make plans that you feel confident about keeping. If something comes up, I would like a heads-up as soon as possible."

Scenario 2: Family Member's Criticism

Script: "I know you care about me, but when you make critical comments about my choices, I feel hurt and defensive. I would appreciate it if we could focus on positive support instead. It means a lot to me to feel encouraged rather than judged."

Scenario 3: Partner Interrupts Conversations

Script: "I love that we can share our thoughts and ideas, but I feel frustrated when I'm interrupted. I would appreciate it if we could take turns speaking so that we both feel heard in our conversations."

Step 3: Role-Play the Scenarios

Find a trusted friend or partner to practice these scripts with. Role-play the scenarios, taking turns being both the person setting the boundary and the person receiving it. This exercise helps you gain confidence in articulating your needs and prepares you for real-life situations.

Step 4: Reflect on Your Experience

After practicing the scenarios, take time to reflect on how it felt to communicate your boundaries. Did you feel empowered? Nervous? Excited? Discuss your feelings with your partner or friend and explore any challenges you faced during the role-play. This reflection can help you identify areas for growth and improvement.

Developing emotional boundaries is essential for nurturing healthy, fulfilling relationships. As you practice setting boundaries with kindness and clarity, you'll find that you are not only protecting your emotional well-being, but also creating space for deeper connections with those around you.

Remember, boundaries are not meant to push people away; rather, they invite respect, understanding, and love into your relationships. By embracing this practice, you're on a journey toward emotional security, healthier attachments, and the joy of authentic connection.

CHAPTER 13

Mindfulness for Healing

In our fast-paced world, where distractions are plentiful and worries often loom large, the practice of mindfulness offers a sanctuary for healing and self-discovery. Mindfulness, the art of being present in the moment can be a powerful tool for transforming attachment patterns and fostering emotional resilience. For those of us navigating the complexities of fearful avoidant attachment, incorporating mindfulness into our daily lives can provide a path toward deeper understanding, acceptance, and connection.

When we practice mindfulness, we cultivate awareness of our thoughts, feelings, and bodily sensations without judgment. This awareness allows us to recognize the patterns that drive our behaviors and emotional responses. By observing our thoughts and feelings as they arise, we can gain insight into how our past experiences influence our present relationships. Mindfulness empowers us to break free from automatic responses rooted in fear and avoidance, creating space for healing and growth.

How Mindfulness Can Transform Attachment Patterns

1. Breaking the Cycle of Automatic Reactions

Fearful avoidant attachment often leads to automatic reactions patterns of behavior that are driven by fear of intimacy or rejection. For example, you might find yourself pulling away from a partner when they get too close, or you might lash out when you feel vulnerable. These reactions are often unconscious, stemming from early experiences that taught you to protect yourself.

Mindfulness provides a way to step back from these automatic reactions. By developing awareness of your thoughts and feelings, you can recognize when these patterns are triggered. Instead of reacting impulsively, you can pause, observe, and choose how to respond. This shift allows you to break the cycle of fear and avoidance, paving the way for healthier, more conscious interactions.

2. Cultivating Self-Compassion

Many individuals with fearful avoidant attachment struggle with self-criticism and feelings of unworthiness. Mindfulness encourages self-compassion,a gentle acceptance of your thoughts and emotions, recognizing that you are human and deserving of kindness, especially in times of struggle.

When you practice mindfulness, you learn to treat yourself with the same compassion you would offer to a friend. Instead of berating yourself for feeling vulnerable or anxious, you can acknowledge these feelings with understanding. This self-compassion creates a foundation for emotional healing and allows you to approach your relationships with greater empathy and patience.

3. Increasing Emotional Awareness
Mindfulness enhances emotional awareness by encouraging you to tune into your emotions as they arise. Many of us tend to avoid uncomfortable feelings, suppressing them until they become overwhelming. This avoidance can lead to emotional outbursts or disconnection in relationships.

Through mindfulness practices, you can learn to observe your emotions without judgment. Instead of pushing them away, you acknowledge their presence and allow yourself to experience them fully. This practice can help you develop a deeper understanding of your emotional landscape, enabling you to respond to your feelings with greater clarity and intention.

4. Fostering Connection

Mindfulness is not just an individual practice; it can also enhance your connections with others. When you are present and attuned to your own emotions, you become more attuned to the emotions of those around you. This heightened awareness allows for deeper, more meaningful interactions, as you can respond to your partner's needs with empathy and understanding.

By practicing mindfulness together with a partner, you can create a shared space of emotional safety. This connection fosters trust and intimacy, helping to heal the wounds that fear and avoidance may have created in your relationship.

<u>10-Minute Mindfulness Practices for Healing</u>

Incorporating mindfulness into your daily routine doesn't have to be complicated or time-consuming. The following exercises can be done in just ten minutes and can help you cultivate mindfulness as a healing practice.

Exercise 1: Mindful Breathing

1. **Find a Comfortable Position**: Sit or lie down in a quiet space where you won't be disturbed. Close your eyes or lower your gaze.
2. **Focus on Your Breath**: Take a deep breath in through your nose, allowing your abdomen to

expand fully. Hold for a moment, then exhale slowly through your mouth.

3. **Count Your Breaths**: Begin to breathe naturally. Count each inhale and exhale up to ten, then start again at one. If your mind wanders, gently bring your focus back to your breath without judgment.

4. **Practice for 5-10 Minutes**: Continue this practice for five to ten minutes, allowing yourself to sink deeper into a state of relaxation and awareness.

Exercise 2: Body Scan

1. **Settle In**: Find a comfortable position, either sitting or lying down. Close your eyes and take a few deep breaths to center yourself.

2. **Bring Awareness to Your Body**: Starting from the top of your head, slowly bring your awareness down through your body. Notice any areas of tension or discomfort.

3. **Release Tension**: As you focus on each part of your body, consciously relax any tension you may be holding. Imagine breathing into those areas, allowing them to soften and release.

4. **Continue Downward**: Move down to your forehead, cheeks, jaw, neck, shoulders, arms, chest, abdomen, legs, and feet. Spend a few moments on each area, bringing awareness and relaxation.

5. **Conclude with Gratitude**: After scanning your body, take a moment to express gratitude for your body and its ability to feel, heal, and connect.

Exercise 3: Mindful Observation

1. **Choose an Object**: Find a small object in your environment, such as a stone, flower, or piece of fruit. Hold it in your hand or place it in front of you.
2. **Observe Mindfully**: Spend a few minutes observing the object. Notice its color, texture, shape, and any other details that stand out.
3. **Engage Your Senses**: If appropriate, engage your sense of smell or touch. Allow yourself to fully immerse in the experience of observing this object without distraction.
4. **Reflect on Your Experience**: After a few minutes, reflect on what you noticed. How did this exercise feel? Did you find your mind wandering? What can you learn from this practice?

As you integrate mindfulness into your life, remember that the goal is not perfection; it's about presence. The more you practice being mindful, the more you cultivate emotional awareness and resilience. This journey allows you to transform your attachment patterns and develop deeper, more meaningful connections with yourself and others.

Mindfulness provides the tools to observe your thoughts and emotions without being consumed by them. It helps you create space for healing, self-acceptance, and growth. Embrace this practice as a powerful ally in your journey toward emotional well-being and relational fulfillment. Through mindfulness, you can rewrite the story of your attachment, transforming fear into trust and disconnection into connection.

CHAPTER 14

Cognitive Behavioral Techniques for Attachment Healing

Understanding and transforming our attachment patterns often requires a deeper look at the thoughts that shape our feelings and behaviors in relationships. Cognitive Behavioral Therapy (CBT) provides powerful tools to help us reframe negative thoughts, challenge limiting beliefs, and create healthier narratives about ourselves and our connections with others. When we learn to recognize and change our thought patterns, we empower ourselves to break free from the chains of fear, insecurity, and avoidance that have held us back.

For those of us with a fearful avoidant attachment style, negative thoughts can often cloud our perceptions of relationships. You might find yourself thinking, "I will never be loved," or "If I get close to someone, I will just end up hurt." These thoughts can lead to behaviors that reinforce your fears, creating a cycle that feels inescapable. However, through the techniques of cognitive behavioral therapy, we can challenge these thoughts and replace them with healthier, more empowering beliefs.

How to Reframe Negative Thoughts Around Relationships

1. Identify Negative Thought Patterns
The first step in reframing negative thoughts is to become aware of them. Take note of the thoughts that arise when you think about relationships or when you find yourself in emotionally charged situations. Are there recurring themes? Common negative thoughts may include:

- *"I always get abandoned."*
- *"I am not worthy of love."*
- *"If I let someone in, they will hurt me."*

Keep a journal where you can write down these thoughts as they arise. This practice will help you recognize patterns and give you insight into how these thoughts influence your emotions and actions.

2. Challenge Your Thoughts
Once you've identified negative thoughts, the next step is to challenge their validity. Ask yourself questions that encourage critical thinking:

- *What evidence do I have to support this thought?*
- *Is there evidence that contradicts this belief?*
- *How would I view this situation if I were giving advice to a friend?*

This process allows you to take a step back from your thoughts and evaluate them more objectively. You might realize that the beliefs you hold are based on past experiences rather than current realities.

3. Reframe Negative Thoughts

After challenging your negative thoughts, the next step is to reframe them into more balanced, constructive statements. This involves shifting your perspective from one of fear and doubt to one of empowerment and possibility. For example:

- *Change "I will never be loved" to "I am worthy of love, and I am learning to open myself to it."*
- *Shift "If I get close to someone, I will get hurt" to "Building connections is a risk, but it also brings the possibility of joy and companionship."*

Reframing helps you create a new narrative that aligns with your values and aspirations, rather than your fears.

4. Practice Self-Compassion

As you work through negative thought patterns, it's important to practice self-compassion. Remember that changing deeply held beliefs takes time and effort. Instead of criticizing yourself for having negative thoughts, acknowledge that it's a natural part of the healing process. Be gentle with yourself, and recognize that you are taking positive steps toward emotional growth.

5. Focus on Action

Reframing thoughts is only part of the process; it's also essential to translate these new beliefs into action. Once you've identified and reframed negative thoughts, think about how you can embody these new beliefs in your behavior. For instance, if you've reframed the belief "I am not worthy of love" to "I am deserving of healthy, fulfilling relationships," consider how you can start taking actions that align with this belief.

This might mean opening up to a friend about your feelings, seeking out new social experiences, or setting healthy boundaries in your relationships. Taking actionable steps reinforces the new narrative and helps create positive change in your life.

Thought Record for Changing Negative Beliefs

The following exercise is designed to help you document, challenge, and reframe negative thoughts that arise around your relationships. This thought record can serve as a valuable tool in your journey toward attachment healing.

Step 1: Create Your Thought Record Template
Set up a simple chart with the following columns:

1. *Date: Write down the date when you noticed the thought.*
2. *Trigger: Identify the situation or event that triggered the negative thought.*
3. *Negative Thought: Record the specific negative thought you experienced.*
4. *Emotions: Write down the emotions you felt in response to the thought (e.g., sadness, anger, anxiety).*
5. *Evidence For: List any evidence that supports this negative thought.*
6. *Evidence Against: Write down any evidence that contradicts the negative thought.*
7. *Reframed Thought: Create a new, balanced thought that reflects a more constructive perspective.*

Step 2: Fill Out Your Thought Record

As you go through your day, pay attention to any negative thoughts that arise, especially in relation to your relationships. When you notice a negative thought, take a moment to fill out your thought record.

For example:

- **Date**: March 1
- **Trigger**: My partner didn't respond to my text right away.
- **Negative Thought**: "They must not care about me."
- **Emotions**: Anxiety, sadness.
- **Evidence For**: They took a long time to reply last week too.
- **Evidence Against**: They are busy with work, and they usually respond when they can. They've told me they care about me.
- **Reframed Thought**: "My partner likely had a good reason for not responding right away. Their feelings for me are genuine."

Step 3: Review and Reflect

At the end of the week, review your thought records. Look for patterns in your negative thoughts. Are there particular triggers that tend to lead to certain beliefs?

Reflect on how reframing these thoughts affect your emotions and behavior. Did you notice a shift in how you felt about yourself or your relationships after challenging and changing these thoughts?

Step 4: Commit to Ongoing Practice
Incorporate this thought record exercise into your weekly routine. The more you practice recognizing and reframing negative thoughts, the more natural the process will become. Over time, you'll develop a more empowering narrative around your relationships, paving the way for healthier connections.

Cognitive behavioral techniques provide invaluable tools for healing attachment wounds and transforming negative thought patterns. By learning to identify, challenge, and reframe these thoughts, you empower yourself to rewrite your relationship narrative.

As you embrace this journey of change, remember that healing is not a linear process. It requires patience, self-compassion, and dedication. By committing to these practices, you cultivate the emotional resilience and strength necessary to create healthier, more fulfilling relationships.

Ultimately, you have the power to change your story. By reframing your thoughts, you open yourself up to the possibility of love, connection, and the joy of authentic relationships free from the shadows of fear and self-doubt

CHAPTER 15

Managing Emotional Triggers

Recognizing and Soothing Triggers in Real Time

Emotions have a way of sneaking up on us. You might be going about your day, and suddenly, without warning, something seemingly small sends you spiraling into anger, anxiety, or sadness. These moments are your emotional triggers. A trigger is any experience, memory, or sensation that causes an intense emotional response. Understanding what sets off these emotional reactions can be one of the most powerful tools for self-awareness and growth.

Triggers often stem from past experiences or unresolved feelings. It could be a word someone says, a situation you find yourself in, or even a smell that reminds you of something long ago. The more we understand our triggers, the better we can respond to them. It's not about avoiding the trigger,because life will always throw things your way,but it's about learning how to handle your emotional reaction in the moment.

The first step in managing emotional triggers is **awareness**. You cannot change what you are unaware of. You have to be able to recognize the moments when a trigger is being set off inside you. This requires mindfulness, a deep sense of presence, and the willingness to step outside of your reactive mind for a moment to observe yourself.

Imagine you're in a heated conversation. The words being spoken are digging into old wounds, and you feel your heart rate spike. At this point, many of us are tempted to lash out or retreat, following old patterns of emotional reaction. But there is another way. **Recognizing** the trigger in real time is like shining a light on it. Once you are aware that you've been triggered, you've already taken the first and most important step towards soothing it.

Take a deep breath. Acknowledge the feeling that's coming up. Give it a name. "I'm feeling angry," "I'm feeling scared," or "I'm feeling hurt." Naming the emotion helps you gain clarity over what you are dealing with. It gives you a bit of space between the trigger and your reaction, allowing you to choose how you want to respond instead of being swept away by it.

Triggers are powerful because they tap into the parts of ourselves that feel vulnerable. They awaken emotions that have often been buried for years. But the beauty of understanding triggers is that you can use these moments as opportunities for healing. Each time you recognize and soothe a trigger, you are rewriting an old story. Instead of reacting out of fear or anger, you are responding with wisdom and compassion, both for yourself and others.

Once you've named the emotion, the next step is to **soothe** it. Emotional triggers are intense, and they pull you into a fight-or-flight state. In these moments, the brain sends signals that tell your body to either prepare for battle or escape the situation. But we are not slaves to these impulses. We have the ability to calm ourselves, even in the middle of an emotional storm.

A powerful technique for soothing emotional triggers is to focus on your **breath**. When you feel triggered, your breath often becomes shallow or rapid, feeding into the body's stress response. Consciously slow down your breathing. Take deep, deliberate breaths, focusing on the rise and fall of your chest. This simple act of controlled breathing sends a signal to your nervous system that it's safe to relax.

Another approach is to bring your **attention** back to the present moment. Triggers often pull you into the past or thrust you into fear of the future. Grounding yourself in the present helps you regain control. You can do this by focusing on something physical in your surroundings, such as the feeling of your feet on the floor or the texture of an object in your hand. This practice, known as grounding, anchors you in the here and now, reducing the power of the trigger.

It's also helpful to have a **mantra** or calming phrase that you can repeat to yourself when you feel triggered. Something as simple as "I am safe" or "I can handle this" can create a sense of calm and reassurance. The words you choose should resonate with you and bring you a sense of peace.

While recognizing and soothing triggers in the moment is important, a key part of managing emotional triggers is also reflecting on them afterward. Once the intensity has passed, take time to **understand** why you were triggered. What was it about the situation that set off such a strong reaction in you? Often, the trigger points to something deeper, an old wound or fear that hasn't been fully addressed.

For example, if you find yourself getting extremely angry when someone interrupts you, ask yourself why. Is it just about the interruption, or is there a deeper story playing out? Maybe it reminds you of times when you felt disrespected or ignored as a child. By connecting the dots, you can begin to understand the root cause of your trigger, which gives you the power to work through it over time.

Emotional triggers can become **teachers**. They show us where we are still hurting, where we need to grow, and where we can become more compassionate with ourselves. Instead of seeing triggers as something to avoid or suppress, you can see them as opportunities for deeper self-awareness and emotional mastery.

Trigger Response Worksheet for Emotional Clarity

Now that you've learned how to recognize and soothe triggers, it's time to put these insights into action. The following worksheet is designed to help you gain clarity around your emotional triggers and develop strategies for managing them in real time. Set aside a quiet moment to reflect on a recent experience when you were triggered and use the questions below to guide your thoughts.

Step 1: Identify the Trigger

- *What happened? (Describe the situation that triggered you.)*

- *How did you feel in that moment? (List the emotions that arose, such as anger, fear, sadness, etc.)*
- *Where did you feel it in your body? (Did you notice physical sensations like tightness in your chest or knots in your stomach?)*

Step 2: Reflect on the Source

- *Why do you think this situation triggered you? (Was it related to a past experience or a particular belief you hold?)*
- *Is there a recurring theme with this trigger? (Do you find that certain situations, people, or words tend to trigger you often?)*

Step 3: Soothe the Trigger

- *What can you do in the moment to soothe yourself when this trigger arises? (Examples: deep breathing, grounding techniques, repeating a calming phrase.)*
- *What soothing phrase or mantra will you use next time? (Write down a calming statement that resonates with you.)*

Step 4: Plan Your Response

- *How would you like to respond the next time you're triggered? (Instead of reacting impulsively, how can you respond with intention and self-compassion?)*

Step 5: Reflect on the Experience

- *After the trigger has passed, take a moment to reflect. Did you notice any patterns or insights about yourself that can help you in the future?*

This worksheet can be revisited whenever you encounter a new emotional trigger. By making this reflection a regular practice, you train yourself to become more aware of your emotions and better equipped to handle them in the moment.

CHAPTER 16

Reclaiming Your Authentic Self

<u>Letting Go of Fear-Based Identities</u>

Who are you when no one is watching? Who are you when you are not worried about meeting expectations or being judged? These questions go deeper than we often allow ourselves to explore. Many of us move through life wearing masks,identities built out of fear rather than truth. We create personas to shield ourselves from rejection, failure, or disappointment. But these fear-based identities only serve to keep us disconnected from our true selves, limiting our potential and joy.

Reclaiming your authentic self begins with understanding that many of the beliefs you hold about yourself were shaped by fear. Fear of not being good enough. Fear of being unloved or abandoned. Fear of failure. These fears become woven into your identity, causing you to make decisions and live in ways that do not reflect your true nature. You might push yourself to succeed in a career that does not align with your passions because you fear disappointing others. Or perhaps you play small in relationships because you fear being vulnerable.

The moment you recognize these fear-based identities is the moment you reclaim your power. You have the ability to let go of these false versions of yourself and step into the fullness of who you really are. But this process requires deep honesty and courage. It is not easy to let go of the safety nets we have built, even when they hold us back. The fear-based identities often feel like home because they are familiar, but they are not where your true self thrives.

The first step in this journey is recognizing where fear is running the show. Take a moment to think about the areas of your life where you feel stuck or unfulfilled. Is it in your career? Your relationships? Your self-image? Ask yourself if fear is guiding your choices in these areas. Are you staying in a job you dislike because you fear taking a risk? Are you avoiding deep connections in your relationships because you fear getting hurt? Are you constantly criticizing yourself because you fear you are not enough?

Once you identify these fear-driven areas, you can begin the process of letting go. Letting go of fear-based identities is about releasing the stories you have told yourself about who you need to be in order to be accepted or loved. It is about embracing the idea that you are enough as you are, without needing to fit into someone else's mold.

One of the most common ways we build fear-based identities is through comparison. We look at what others are doing and feel like we need to match their level of success, happiness, or appearance. But comparison is a thief of authenticity. It robs you of the ability to see your own unique path and gifts. When you stop comparing yourself to others, you create space to reconnect with what truly matters to you.

Another key aspect of reclaiming your authentic self is recognizing the role of perfectionism. Many of us wear perfectionism like a badge of honor, thinking it will protect us from criticism or failure. But perfectionism is just another form of fear. It keeps you locked in a cycle of never feeling good enough, always striving for an impossible standard. Letting go of perfectionism allows you to embrace your imperfections and see them as part of what makes you authentically human.

As you begin to let go of fear-based identities, you might feel a sense of loss or uncertainty. It can be uncomfortable to step away from the version of yourself that you have held onto for so long. But remember, this is not about losing yourself,it is about finding yourself. The true you has always been there, waiting to be rediscovered beneath the layers of fear and conditioning.

This process of reclaiming your authentic self is not something that happens overnight. It requires ongoing reflection and a willingness to be vulnerable with yourself. But with each step, you will find a greater sense of freedom, joy, and alignment with your true purpose. You will no longer feel the need to conform to others' expectations or live in fear of rejection. Instead, you will move through life with confidence, knowing that you are living in alignment with who you truly are.

Self-Discovery Journaling for Authenticity

To help you on your journey of reclaiming your authentic self, I encourage you to engage in a self-discovery journaling exercise. Journaling allows you to explore your thoughts and feelings in a safe and private space, giving you the clarity and insight needed to break free from fear-based identities. Set aside time to reflect on the following prompts and write honestly, without judgment.

Step 1: Identifying Fear-Based Identities

- *Think about the roles you play in your life (e.g., employee, parent, friend, partner). In which of these roles do you feel like you are not being fully authentic? Why?*

- *What fears come up when you think about being your true self in these roles? Are you afraid of being judged, rejected, or failing?*
- *How have these fear-based identities impacted your life? What have they cost you in terms of happiness, fulfillment, or peace?*

Step 2: Releasing the Fear

- *Write about a time when you acted out of fear rather than authenticity. What was the situation, and how did you feel afterward?*
- *What would it look like to let go of this fear and act from a place of authenticity? How might your life change if you released this fear-based identity?*
- *List three things you can do to start releasing the fear in one specific area of your life. For example, if you fear speaking up in meetings at work, one step might be to voice your opinion in a small, low-risk setting.*

Step 3: Embracing Your Authentic Self

- *What does it mean to you to be authentic? How would you describe your true self?*
- *Reflect on a time when you felt truly aligned with your authentic self. What were you doing, and how did it feel?*

- *Write a letter to your authentic self, affirming your commitment to live in alignment with who you truly are. In this letter, express any fears or doubts you may have, but also acknowledge the power and strength that comes from embracing your true self.*

Step 4: Moving Forward

- *Identify one area of your life where you will make a conscious effort to show up more authentically. What specific actions can you take to live in alignment with your true self in this area?*
- *Set a daily or weekly intention to check in with yourself and ask, "Am I acting out of fear, or am I acting from my authentic self?" Use this as a tool to guide your decisions and actions moving forward.*
- *Consider sharing your journey with a trusted friend or mentor. Sometimes, talking about your experiences can provide additional insight and accountability.*

Reclaiming your authentic self is one of the most liberating journeys you can embark on. It is about shedding the layers of fear and conditioning that have kept you from fully embracing who you are. As you let go of these fear-based identities, you will discover a deeper sense of peace, purpose, and connection with yourself and the world around you. You will no longer feel the need to perform or please others, because you will know that who you are at your core is more than enough.

> *This process takes time, and it will not always be easy. But as you continue to show up for yourself, to recognize where fear is holding you back, and to choose authenticity over fear, you will find that the rewards are immeasurable. You will feel more alive, more at peace, and more empowered to live the life that is truly meant for you.*

The world does not need more people who are simply fitting in. It needs people who are brave enough to be themselves, fully and unapologetically. You are one of those people. You have the courage, the wisdom, and the strength to reclaim your authentic self, and in doing so, you give others permission to do the same.

So, take that first step today. Let go of the fear, embrace who you truly are, and reclaim the life that is yours to live. The world is waiting for the real you.

CHAPTER 17

The Power of Self-Compassion

How Self-Compassion Fuels Attachment Healing

Many of us are taught early on to be hard on ourselves. We are told that self-criticism is the key to success, that if we are not pushing ourselves relentlessly, we will fall short. But what if this approach is not only unnecessary but also harmful to our well-being? What if the very thing we need most, especially when healing deep wounds, is not harsh judgment, but compassion?

Self-compassion is the quiet yet transformative force that has the power to reshape our relationship with ourselves. It is the simple act of offering ourselves the kindness we so easily extend to others. This might sound too simple to be profound, but the truth is, it is life-changing. Especially when it comes to attachment healing, self-compassion is the missing link that helps us break free from the patterns of fear and disconnection that we have been trapped in for so long.

Attachment wounds are often formed when we do not receive the love, care, or validation we needed in our early years. These wounds can leave us feeling unworthy, anxious, or disconnected from others. And the way we treat ourselves often reflects these deep-seated beliefs. We may criticize ourselves harshly, believing that if we could just be "better," more worthy of love, we could heal. But in truth, healing begins with softening,softening toward ourselves, toward the parts of us that feel broken or inadequate.

Self-compassion is not about excusing harmful behaviors or ignoring areas where we need to grow. It is about approaching ourselves with understanding rather than judgment. It is about recognizing that, just like everyone else, we are doing the best we can with what we have. And sometimes, the hardest person to show compassion to is ourselves.

When you begin practicing self-compassion, you start to create a safe internal space where healing can happen. The harsh inner critic that tells you that you are not good enough begins to lose its power. In its place, a gentler voice emerges,the voice of understanding, of patience, and of love. This shift is profound because it changes the way you relate to yourself, especially in moments of struggle.

Attachment healing requires us to rewrite the stories we have been telling ourselves for years. These stories might sound like, "I am unlovable," or "People always leave," or "I have to be perfect to be accepted." These beliefs have deep roots, often planted in early childhood when we did not feel safe or loved in the ways we needed. But as adults, we have the power to change these narratives, and self-compassion is the tool that makes this possible.

By offering yourself compassion, you are giving yourself the love and validation you may not have received in the past. You are showing yourself that you are worthy of care, even in moments of difficulty. This practice helps to heal attachment wounds because it addresses the core issue: the belief that you are not enough as you are. Self-compassion teaches you that you are enough, exactly as you are, flaws and all.

Imagine a moment when you are feeling anxious or overwhelmed. In these moments, it is easy to spiral into self-criticism. "Why can't I handle this better? What is wrong with me?" But what if, instead of criticizing yourself, you paused and asked, "What do I need right now?" This simple shift,asking yourself what you need instead of what you did wrong,opens the door to healing. It allows you to respond to your pain with care rather than judgment.

Self-compassion is not just a practice for when things go wrong. It is also about how you treat yourself on a daily basis. It is about speaking kindly to yourself when you wake up in the morning, about offering yourself patience when you make a mistake, and about recognizing that you, like every other human being, are deserving of love and respect.

This shift in mindset is especially important in the context of attachment healing because our early relationships shape the way we relate to ourselves. If you grew up in an environment where love was conditional, where you had to be "good" or "perfect" to receive affection, then you likely learned to withhold love from yourself unless you met certain standards. Self-compassion undoes this conditioning by teaching you that love is not something you have to earn. It is something you deserve simply because you exist.

As you practice self-compassion, you begin to cultivate a sense of security within yourself. You realize that you can be your own source of comfort and care, rather than relying on others to provide what you never received. This does not mean you do not need others, we are all wired for connection, but it means that your self-worth is no longer dependent on external validation. You learn to trust yourself, to hold yourself with the same kindness you would offer a friend, and this creates the foundation for healthy, secure relationships with others.

Self-compassion also plays a crucial role in breaking the cycle of shame. Shame is often at the root of attachment wounds, convincing us that we are fundamentally flawed or unworthy. When we approach ourselves with compassion, we begin to dismantle this shame. We recognize that making mistakes, feeling insecure, or struggling does not mean we are unworthy,it simply means we are human.

By treating yourself with compassion, you create a safe space within yourself where shame cannot thrive. You begin to rewrite the story of who you are, not as someone who is broken or deficient, but as someone who is whole, worthy, and deserving of love. This shift in perspective is what fuels attachment healing. It allows you to step out of old patterns of fear, insecurity, and self-criticism, and into a new way of being,one that is grounded in love, acceptance, and compassion for yourself.

Guided Self-Compassion Practice

Now that we have explored the power of self-compassion, it is time to put this wisdom into practice. The following guided exercise will help you cultivate self-compassion in your daily life. Set aside some time in a quiet, comfortable space where you can focus without distractions. This exercise can be done as a journaling practice or simply as a mental reflection.

Step 1: Identify a Moment of Struggle

- *Begin by recalling a recent moment when you felt overwhelmed, anxious, or self-critical. It could be something small, like getting frustrated at work, or something more significant, like feeling unworthy in a relationship.*
- *Take a few deep breaths and bring this moment to mind, allowing yourself to fully experience the emotions that came up. Do not push the feelings away, just observe them without judgment.*

Step 2: Acknowledge the Pain

- *Now, gently acknowledge that this is a moment of difficulty. Say to yourself, "This is hard," or "I am struggling right now." Recognizing your pain is the first step toward offering yourself compassion.*
- *Remind yourself that struggling is part of the human experience. You are not alone in feeling this way. Everyone experiences pain, failure, and insecurity at times.*

Step 3: Offer Yourself Kindness

- *Imagine what you would say to a close friend who was going through the same struggle. You would likely offer them words of comfort, understanding, and support. Now, offer those same words to yourself. It might feel unfamiliar at first, but let yourself receive kindness.*

- *Say to yourself, "I am here for you," or "You are doing the best you can." Use whatever words feel soothing and supportive to you.*

Step 4: Ask What You Need

- *Take a moment to ask yourself, "What do I need right now?" Maybe you need rest, reassurance, or simply a break from the pressure you are feeling. Whatever the answer is, honor it. This is a powerful way to show yourself that your needs matter.*

Step 5: Let Go of Self-Judgment

- *If you find yourself slipping into self-criticism during this exercise, gently remind yourself that being kind to yourself does not mean you are letting yourself off the hook. It means you are choosing to respond to yourself with care rather than judgment.*
- *Repeat the phrase, "I am human, and it is okay to struggle." Allow this truth to sink in as you release any harsh judgments you have been holding onto.*

Self-compassion is not just a practice,it is a way of being. It is a way of showing up for yourself with the love, care, and understanding that you deserve. As you cultivate self-compassion, you begin to heal the wounds that have kept you from fully embracing who you are. You learn to treat yourself with the same kindness you offer to others, and in doing so, you reclaim your sense of worth and wholeness.

Attachment healing is not a quick fix; it is a journey. But with self-compassion as your guide, you can navigate this journey with grace, knowing that every step you take is a step toward greater healing and peace. As you continue to practice self-compassion, you will find that the walls you have built around your heart begin to soften. You will become more open to love,both from yourself and from others. And in this openness, you will discover the truth: that you have always been worthy of love, exactly as you are.

CHAPTER 18

Rebuilding Trust in Yourself

<u>How to Trust Yourself in Relationships Again</u>

One of the most challenging aspects of emotional recovery is learning to trust yourself again. Life's disappointments, betrayals, and mistakes can erode the trust you once had in your own judgment. This loss of trust often leads to doubt, fear, and indecision, especially in relationships. You may find yourself constantly second-guessing your feelings, your choices, and your ability to navigate relationships in a healthy way. But the truth is, rebuilding trust in yourself is not just possible, it is essential for deep, meaningful connections with others.

At its core, self-trust is about believing that you can handle whatever life throws at you. It is about knowing that no matter what happens, you have the strength, resilience, and wisdom to respond in a way that honors your well-being. Trusting yourself is not about being perfect or never making mistakes,it is about knowing that even when things go wrong, you can find your way back to balance.

The breakdown of self-trust often starts in relationships, especially if you have experienced betrayal, manipulation, or emotional neglect. When someone you cared about deeply lets you down, it is easy to start questioning not just their motives, but your own judgment. "How could I not have seen the signs?" "Why did I let this happen?" These are the questions that start to play in your mind, and before you know it, you are doubting your ability to make sound decisions.

But here's the reality: Trusting yourself does not mean you will never be hurt or deceived again. It means that even if someone betrays you, you will be able to recover and move forward. Self-trust gives you the strength to recognize that while others' actions are beyond your control, your response is not. You always have the power to choose how you react to the world around you.

Rebuilding trust in yourself starts with self-awareness. You need to understand where the doubts come from, and often, these doubts are rooted in fear. Fear of making the wrong choice, fear of being vulnerable, fear of repeating past mistakes. These fears can paralyze you, keeping you from fully engaging in relationships or making decisions that truly reflect your desires. To begin rebuilding trust in yourself, you need to acknowledge these fears without letting them control you.

Ask yourself, "What am I afraid will happen if I trust myself?" The answer may reveal that you are afraid of failure, rejection, or disappointment. But remember, these experiences are a part of life, not a reflection of your worth or your ability to make sound decisions. Learning to trust yourself again means accepting that life comes with uncertainties, but that does not mean you are ill-equipped to handle them.

A powerful way to begin rebuilding self-trust is through the practice of **self-forgiveness**. Often, the reason we lose trust in ourselves is because we are holding onto past mistakes. We punish ourselves for decisions that did not turn out the way we hoped, replaying moments where we feel we "should have known better." But the truth is, you are human, and being human means you will make mistakes. Instead of criticizing yourself for the times you fell short, can you forgive yourself? Can you recognize that you were doing the best you could with the information and tools you had at the time?

Self-forgiveness is not about excusing harmful behavior or ignoring the consequences of your actions. It is about releasing the harsh judgment that keeps you stuck in a cycle of self-doubt. By forgiving yourself, you free up the emotional space to learn from your experiences and move forward with more wisdom and clarity.

Another key element in rebuilding trust in yourself is learning to **listen to your intuition**. Your intuition is that quiet inner voice that often knows what you need before your mind has a chance to analyze it. The problem is, many of us have become disconnected from this inner guidance system. We are so accustomed to looking outside of ourselves for validation,seeking approval from others, following societal expectations,that we have lost touch with our own inner compass.

To rebuild trust in yourself, you need to reconnect with your intuition. This means giving yourself permission to trust your gut feelings, even when they go against logic or the opinions of others. Start by paying attention to how your body feels in certain situations. Do you feel a sense of ease or tension? Do you feel expansive or contracted? Your body often holds the answers you are looking for, and by tuning in, you can begin to make decisions that are aligned with your true self.

Of course, trusting your intuition does not mean ignoring reason or disregarding facts. It is about finding a balance between your inner wisdom and the information available to you. When you learn to trust both your mind and your intuition, you become a more confident and grounded decision-maker.

Rebuilding trust in yourself also involves setting **boundaries**. When you have clear boundaries, you demonstrate to yourself that your needs and feelings matter. Boundaries are not about keeping people out,they are about protecting your emotional and mental space. They help you stay connected to your values and prevent you from overextending yourself or compromising your well-being for the sake of others.

Trusting yourself means trusting that you know what is best for you, even when others disagree. This is not about being stubborn or refusing to listen to advice,it is about recognizing that at the end of the day, you are the one who has to live with the consequences of your decisions. Setting boundaries allows you to honor your own needs and make choices that reflect your highest good.

Lastly, rebuilding self-trust requires **patience and practice**. This is not something that happens overnight. Just as trust is built over time in relationships with others, it takes time to rebuild trust with yourself. Be patient with yourself as you go through this process. There will be moments of doubt, and that is okay. What matters is that you continue to show up for yourself, even when it feels difficult.

Trust is built in small moments,each time you make a decision that honors your needs, each time you listen to your intuition, and each time you forgive yourself for being human, you are rebuilding that trust. Over time, these small acts add up, and before you know it, you will find that you no longer question your ability to make choices or navigate relationships. You will know, deep down, that you are capable, resilient, and worthy of your own trust.

Trust-Building Practices for Personal Growth

To help you strengthen trust in yourself, try the following trust-building exercises. These practices are designed to help you reconnect with your intuition, honor your needs, and rebuild the trust that may have been lost over time.

Step 1: Daily Check-In

- *Start each day by checking in with yourself. Take a few moments to sit quietly and ask yourself, "How am I feeling today? What do I need?" Allow yourself to tune into your emotions and physical sensations without judgment.*
- *Write down what comes up. This could be as simple as needing more rest, or as complex as feeling anxious about an upcoming decision. The goal is to develop a habit of listening to yourself and honoring your feelings.*

Step 2: Trust Your Small Decisions

- *Practice trusting yourself in small, everyday decisions. Whether it is choosing what to eat, deciding how to spend your free time, or picking out an outfit, make these decisions based on what feels right to you at the moment.*
- *Resist the urge to second-guess yourself. Instead, remind yourself that there is no "right" or "wrong" choice, only the choice that feels most aligned with your needs and desires at that moment.*

Step 3: Reflect on Past Successes

- *Take time to reflect on moments in your life where you trusted yourself and it paid off. These could be small victories or significant decisions where following your intuition led to positive outcomes.*
- *Write these down in a journal. When you start to doubt yourself, revisit these entries to remind yourself that you are capable of making good decisions and navigating challenges.*

Step 4: Set and Honor Boundaries

- *Identify one area in your life where you need to set a boundary. This could be in a relationship, at work, or even with yourself (for example, limiting screen time before bed).*

- *Practice setting and honoring this boundary, and notice how it feels. Pay attention to any discomfort or guilt that comes up, but also notice the sense of empowerment that comes from protecting your well-being.*

Step 5: Self-Forgiveness Ritual

- *Choose a past mistake or decision that you are holding onto. Write it down, along with any self-critical thoughts you have about it.*
- *Now, write a letter of forgiveness to yourself. In this letter, acknowledge that you made the best decision you could with the information you had at the time. Offer yourself kindness and understanding, just as you would to a close friend who made a mistake.*
- *After writing the letter, perform a simple ritual to symbolize letting go. This could be tearing up the letter, burning it, or placing it in a special box. The goal is to release the burden of self-judgment and make space for trust to grow.*

Rebuilding trust in yourself is one of the most empowering and transformative things you can do. It frees you from the constant doubt, second-guessing, and fear that may have held you back for years. When you trust yourself, you step into your full power,you become the author of your own life, no longer relying on others to validate your worth or make decisions for you.

This journey is not without its challenges, but with patience, practice, and self-compassion, you will find that each step brings you closer to a deeper sense of confidence and inner peace. Trusting yourself is not just about making the right decisions,it is about knowing that even when things go wrong, you have the strength, resilience, and wisdom to navigate through it.

As you continue to rebuild trust in yourself, you will notice that your relationships with others also begin to improve. When you trust yourself, you show up more fully and authentically in your interactions. You no longer need to seek approval or fear rejection because you know, at your core, that you are enough.

So take a deep breath, trust that you are on the right path, and continue to show up for yourself each day. The more you practice, the stronger your self-trust will become, and the more aligned your life will be with the truth of who you are.

CHAPTER 19

Creating Secure and Fulfilling Connections

Steps to Form Meaningful and Lasting Bonds

At the heart of human life is connection,the deep, meaningful bonds we form with others that bring us joy, fulfillment, and a sense of belonging. Yet, creating truly secure and lasting connections can be one of the most challenging endeavors we face. Many of us carry the wounds of past relationships, which can make trusting and opening up to others feel like a risk. However, it is through these connections that we grow, heal, and experience the fullness of life.

To create secure and fulfilling connections, we must first understand what makes a bond truly meaningful. It is not about perfection, constant agreement, or avoiding conflict. Rather, it is about cultivating a foundation of trust, vulnerability, and mutual respect. Secure connections are built on the ability to be your true self while allowing the other person to do the same. When both people feel seen, heard, and valued, the relationship naturally deepens.

The first step to forming meaningful bonds is to **cultivate self-awareness**. Before you can connect deeply with someone else, you need to understand your own emotional landscape. What are your fears, your desires, your triggers? How do you react in moments of vulnerability? Knowing yourself is the key to showing up authentically in relationships, and it also helps you recognize when old patterns of fear or insecurity are interfering with your ability to connect.

Self-awareness also allows you to identify your **attachment style**, which plays a major role in how you form and maintain relationships. People with secure attachment styles tend to trust easily and communicate openly, while those with anxious or avoidant attachment styles may struggle with fear of abandonment or fear of intimacy. Understanding your attachment style helps you navigate your relationship dynamics and gives you the tools to heal any patterns that are keeping you from experiencing deeper connection.

Once you are aware of your own emotional needs and patterns, the next step is to **create a space of emotional safety** in your relationships. Emotional safety means that both people feel free to express themselves without fear of judgment, criticism, or rejection. This kind of safety is the foundation of any secure bond, as it allows both individuals to be vulnerable. Vulnerability is essential for deep connection because it requires trust. When you open up and share your innermost thoughts, fears, and desires, you invite the other person to do the same, creating a bond that goes beyond surface-level interaction.

Building emotional safety starts with **active listening**. So often in conversations, we are thinking about how we are going to respond instead of truly hearing what the other person is saying. Active listening means being fully present, without distraction, and showing the other person that their words matter. It means listening not just to respond, but to understand. When you listen in this way, you make the other person feel valued and respected, which strengthens the bond between you.

Another important aspect of building meaningful connections is **emotional attunement**. This means being aware of and responding to the emotions of the other person, even when they are not directly expressed. Sometimes, a person may not have the words to explain what they are feeling, but by being attuned to their body language, tone of voice, or facial expressions, you can pick up on the emotions beneath the surface. Emotional attunement creates a sense of being deeply understood, which is essential for lasting bonds.

Trust is the cornerstone of secure relationships. Without trust, no relationship can truly thrive. But trust is not built overnight; it is developed through consistent actions over time. To build trust, you must be reliable, honest, and transparent. Trust grows when you follow through on your commitments, when you show up consistently, and when you are honest,even when it is difficult. Trust also means giving the other person the benefit of the doubt, assuming good intentions, and offering forgiveness when mistakes are made.

In addition to trust, **mutual respect** is crucial for forming meaningful connections. Respect goes beyond simple courtesy,it is about honoring the other person's boundaries, needs, and individuality. In secure relationships, both people feel respected for who they are, without pressure to change or conform. This kind of respect allows the relationship to grow naturally, without fear of judgment or rejection.

Another essential element of deep connection is **shared vulnerability**. Vulnerability is often seen as a weakness, but in truth, it is a strength. When you allow yourself to be vulnerable, you invite deeper intimacy. Being open about your fears, desires, and insecurities creates a space for the other person to do the same. It is in these moments of shared vulnerability that the most meaningful bonds are formed. However, vulnerability should be met with care and empathy. If someone shares something deeply personal, respond with compassion, not judgment.

Conflict is inevitable in any relationship, but how you handle it can either strengthen or weaken the bond. In secure relationships, conflict is seen as an opportunity for growth, not a threat to the connection. When disagreements arise, approach them with the mindset of understanding rather than winning. Use "I" statements to express your feelings without blaming or attacking the other person. For example, instead of saying, "You never listen to me," try saying, "I feel unheard when I try to express my thoughts." This approach fosters understanding and prevents defensiveness.

Finally, creating lasting connections requires **mutual effort and investment**. Relationships are like gardens,they need to be tended to regularly in order to thrive. This means making time for the other person, showing appreciation, and putting in the effort to maintain the bond. Relationships cannot be one-sided. Both people must be willing to invest their time, energy, and love into the connection. When both individuals are committed to nurturing the relationship, it becomes a source of strength, joy, and fulfillment.

Intimacy-Building Exercises for Deeper Relationships

To help you cultivate secure and fulfilling connections, try these intimacy-building exercises. These practices are designed to deepen your emotional connection with others and foster a sense of closeness and trust.

Step 1: The Vulnerability Share

- *Set aside time with someone close to you, whether it is a partner, friend, or family member, for a deep conversation. Begin by agreeing to share something personal,whether it is a fear, a regret, or a dream that you have not talked about before.*
- *Take turns sharing, and as each person speaks, the other listens without interrupting or offering solutions. Simply hold space for the other person's vulnerability.*
- *After both of you have shared, reflect on how it felt to be open and to listen deeply. Notice if you feel more connected after the exercise.*

Step 2: The Gratitude Practice

- *For one week, make a point to express gratitude to the people in your life. Whether it is a simple thank you for something small or a more heartfelt acknowledgment of their support, this practice helps to strengthen the bond by showing appreciation.*
- *At the end of the week, take note of how expressing gratitude has impacted your*

relationships. Often, this simple act of appreciation can deepen emotional closeness and make the other person feel valued.

Step 3: Non-Verbal Connection

- *In relationships, words are not the only way to communicate. Physical touch, eye contact, and gestures can also convey deep emotional connection.*
- *Take time to connect non-verbally with someone close to you. This could be holding hands, maintaining eye contact during a conversation, or offering a comforting hug when words are not needed.*
- *Reflect on how these non-verbal forms of connection make you feel and how they strengthen the bond between you.*

Step 4: Emotional Check-In

- *Set aside regular time for an emotional check-in with your partner or close friend. During these check-ins, ask each other how you are feeling emotionally and mentally. Share any concerns or feelings that have come up since your last check-in.*
- *This practice helps prevent small issues from building up into larger problems and creates a*

space for open and honest communication. It also fosters emotional intimacy by allowing both people to feel heard and understood.

Step 5: The Joint Project

- *Working on something together can strengthen your connection. Choose a project, whether it is cooking a meal, planning a trip, or creating something artistic, and collaborate with your partner or friend.*
- *As you work together, pay attention to how you communicate and how your dynamic evolves. The shared effort fosters a sense of partnership and can deepen the bond through cooperation and mutual accomplishment.*

Creating secure and fulfilling connections requires intention, vulnerability, and mutual effort. It is about showing up authentically, listening deeply, and building trust through consistent actions. It is about creating a space where both people feel seen, heard, and valued for who they truly are. These connections, built on trust, respect, and emotional safety, become the foundation for deep and lasting relationships.

As you engage in the intimacy-building practices outlined in this chapter, you will notice that your relationships begin to take on a new depth. You will experience a sense of closeness and security that comes from being vulnerable and allowing others to do the same. Remember, the strongest connections are not those that are free from conflict or difficulty, but those where both people are committed to growing and supporting each other through all of life's ups and downs.

Whether you are building new relationships or deepening existing ones, the key is to show up with an open heart, a willingness to be vulnerable, and a commitment to mutual respect and understanding. In doing so, you create the foundation for bonds that are not only secure and fulfilling but truly life-changing.

CHAPTER 20

Overcoming Setbacks on the Path to Healing

<u>Why Relapses Happen and How to Recover</u>

Healing, whether it's emotional, mental, or physical, is rarely a straight line. You may have moments where everything feels clear, and you're moving forward with strength and clarity. And then suddenly, out of nowhere, you stumble. The progress you made feels distant, and the old patterns, thoughts, or habits you thought you had left behind reappear. This experience is what many refer to as a "relapse." But here's something you may not have heard before: setbacks are not a sign of failure. They are a part of the process.

In the journey to heal and grow, setbacks and relapses are not only common, they are expected. The idea that progress should be smooth and linear is misleading and sets up unrealistic expectations. Real growth comes with challenges, and those challenges are what test and ultimately strengthen the healing you've been working toward. The key is not to avoid setbacks but to learn how to navigate them when they arise, so they don't derail your progress entirely.

To truly understand why relapses happen, we need to look at the brain's patterns and habits. Your mind is wired to follow familiar routes, and even when you are working hard to break a pattern,like negative thinking, fear-based reactions, or self-sabotaging behaviors,those old pathways are still there. They don't disappear overnight. Stress, fatigue, or unexpected triggers can cause you to fall back into these old patterns because they are what your brain knows best. This is not a reflection of your willpower or strength; it's simply how the human mind works.

Relapses often happen when you are overwhelmed, when you are tired, or when you're facing a difficult situation that feels similar to something you have experienced in the past. These moments activate the old survival mechanisms that are still present within you. Instead of seeing this as a failure, recognize it for what it is: an invitation to revisit and strengthen the work you have already started. Every setback is an opportunity to deepen your healing and learn more about yourself.

One of the most important things you can do when you experience a setback is to **practice self-compassion**. Too often, when we stumble, we become our own harshest critic. The voice in your head might say things like, "I can't believe I did this again," or "I'm never going to get better." But this self-criticism only makes the relapse worse. Instead of beating yourself up, offer yourself the same kindness and understanding you would give to a friend who is struggling. A setback doesn't erase your progress; it's a moment that needs to be met with patience, not judgment.

In fact, **setbacks are moments of growth**. It is through these challenges that you develop the resilience to move forward. Each time you recover from a relapse, you are building emotional muscles that make you stronger, more capable, and more self-aware. The next time a similar challenge arises, you will have more tools, more wisdom, and more confidence to handle it.

The first step in recovering from a setback is **acknowledgment**. Recognize that you've had a difficult moment, and that's okay. Healing isn't about never struggling again; it's about learning to recover more quickly and with more grace each time you fall. Once you acknowledge what has happened, take a moment to reflect on the situation. What were the circumstances that led to the setback? Was there a specific trigger,an argument, stress at work, or an emotional situation,that caused you to fall back into old habits? Understanding the context of your relapse can help you avoid similar triggers in the future or prepare for them differently.

Next, focus on **reframing the experience**. Instead of viewing the relapse as a failure, see it as a moment to practice the tools you've been developing. Ask yourself, "What can I learn from this?" Maybe you'll realize that you need more rest or that you need to set better boundaries in certain relationships. Maybe you'll discover that there are still areas of your life that require more healing and attention. Whatever the lesson, use it as fuel for growth rather than a reason to give up.

A key part of overcoming setbacks is **reconnecting with your support system**. Healing isn't something you have to do alone. Reach out to trusted friends, family, or a therapist who can offer perspective, encouragement, and a reminder of the progress you have already made. Sometimes, all it takes is an outside voice to remind you that one misstep doesn't define your journey.

Another essential practice when facing a setback is **returning to your core practices**,the things that have been helping you on your healing path. This might be meditation, journaling, exercise, or spending time in nature. When you experience a relapse, it's easy to forget the very things that support your well-being. The key is to gently guide yourself back to these practices, even if it feels difficult at first. Slowly but surely, they will help you regain your footing.

It's also important to **set realistic expectations** for your healing journey. The desire to heal quickly and completely can create a lot of internal pressure, but healing isn't about speed. It's about depth. There will be layers to your healing process, and sometimes, a relapse is simply the uncovering of a deeper layer that needs attention. By setting realistic expectations, you allow yourself the grace to move through each phase of healing without the added burden of feeling like you need to "get it right" every time.

When you experience a setback, it's also helpful to **revisit your progress**. Take a moment to reflect on how far you've come. Often, we are so focused on where we want to go that we forget to acknowledge the progress we've already made. Looking back on past victories, no matter how small, can remind you that setbacks are just part of a larger process of growth and transformation.

Lastly, one of the most powerful tools for overcoming setbacks is **forgiveness**. Not just forgiveness for others who may have contributed to your relapse, but forgiveness for yourself. Healing is not about being perfect. It's about being human. And being human means you will have moments where you fall short. The most important thing you can do is to forgive yourself for those moments, learn from them, and move forward with more love and understanding for who you are.

Reflective Practices for Handling Setbacks

To help you navigate setbacks with more ease and grace, here is a reflective practice designed to guide you through these challenging moments. This exercise will help you gain clarity, find compassion, and create a plan for moving forward.

Step 1: Acknowledge the Setback

- *Take a moment to sit quietly and reflect on the setback you experienced. What happened? How did you feel? What was the trigger or situation that led to this moment?*
- *Write down your thoughts in a journal. Acknowledging the setback is the first step toward understanding it. Be gentle with yourself as you write, avoiding self-criticism.*

Step 2: Identify the Lesson

- *Now, reflect on what you can learn from this experience. What is the setback teaching you about yourself, your healing process, or your needs?*
- *Write down at least one lesson you can take away from this moment. It might be something as simple as recognizing that you need more*

self-care or that certain situations still trigger old patterns.

Step 3: Reconnect with Support

- *Reach out to a trusted friend, therapist, or loved one. Share your experience with them, and allow them to offer their support and perspective. Sometimes, hearing another person's encouragement can help you see the situation more clearly.*
- *If you prefer not to reach out to someone else, take time to reflect on the people in your life who support your healing. Remind yourself that you are not alone in this journey.*

Step 4: Revisit Your Core Practices

- *What practices have been helping you on your healing path? Whether it's meditation, exercise, journaling, or simply taking quiet moments for yourself, now is the time to return to those practices.*
- *Commit to engaging in one of these practices today. Even if it's just for a few minutes, returning to the routines that support your well-being will help you regain your sense of balance.*

Step 5: Practice Self-Compassion

- *Take a moment to offer yourself compassion. Place your hand on your heart and repeat the following affirmation: "I am human, and it's okay to struggle. I am learning and growing with every experience."*
- *Allow yourself to feel the warmth of your own kindness. Remember that setbacks are not a reflection of your worth or your ability to heal.*

Step 6: Plan for Moving Forward

- *What steps can you take to move forward from this setback? Write down one or two small actions that will help you regain your momentum. These could be simple actions like setting aside time for self-care, journaling about your feelings, or talking to a friend about your experience.*
- *Focus on small, manageable steps rather than overwhelming yourself with big goals. The key is to keep moving forward, even if it's just one small step at a time.*

Setbacks are not the end of your healing journey; they are a part of it. Every relapse, every misstep, is an opportunity to grow stronger, wiser, and more compassionate toward yourself. The path to healing is not about never falling,it's about learning how to get back up, again and again, with more grace, more understanding, and more love for who you are becoming.

By approaching setbacks with self-compassion, patience, and a willingness to learn, you transform these moments of struggle into stepping stones toward deeper healing. Remember, healing is not about perfection. It is about embracing the full spectrum of your experience,both the highs and the lows,and trusting that every part of the journey is leading you toward wholeness.

So, the next time you face a setback, remind yourself that this is not a sign of failure. It is a sign that you are growing, that you are human, and that you are capable of navigating whatever challenges come your way. Keep moving forward, with compassion in your heart and the knowledge that each step, no matter how small, is taking you closer to the healing and peace you deserve.

CHAPTER 21

Embodying Emotional Freedom

Living as Your Secure, Authentic Self

Emotional freedom is one of the most profound gifts you can give yourself. It is the state of living fully in alignment with who you are, free from the chains of fear, self-doubt, and the need for external validation. It is about trusting yourself completely,your emotions, your decisions, your boundaries,and allowing those truths to guide you, rather than being swayed by the opinions, judgments, or expectations of others. This is what it means to live as your secure, authentic self.

But how do you truly embody emotional freedom? Many people think emotional freedom means being untouched by life's ups and downs, never feeling pain or discomfort again. But that's not the case. Living as your authentic self doesn't mean avoiding life's difficulties,it means navigating them with a deep sense of security and trust in yourself. It is the understanding that you have the strength, wisdom, and emotional resilience to handle whatever life throws your way.

The journey to emotional freedom starts with recognizing where you've been holding yourself back. We often build walls around ourselves in response to pain, rejection, or fear. These walls might look like emotional numbness, people-pleasing, or constant self-criticism. They might show up as patterns of perfectionism, avoiding vulnerability, or staying in situations that no longer serve you because you fear the unknown. These walls are built from past experiences that taught you it wasn't safe to be yourself,experiences that told you you needed to protect yourself by hiding who you truly are.

But here is the truth: emotional freedom comes when you dismantle those walls. It's about releasing the outdated beliefs and stories that no longer serve you, and trusting that it is safe to be who you truly are. Emotional freedom doesn't mean that you'll never feel fear or doubt again,it means you won't let those emotions control your actions or define your worth.

The first step to embodying emotional freedom is **acknowledging your true self**. Many of us spend years living with a version of ourselves shaped by others' expectations,parents, society, partners, or friends. We lose touch with our own desires, our own voice, in the process. To live freely, you need to reconnect with that inner voice. Ask yourself: What do I truly want? What makes me feel alive? What am I passionate about? These questions help you return to the essence of who you are.

Living authentically also means honoring your emotions. In our society, we're often told to push down feelings that are uncomfortable,sadness, anger, disappointment, fear,as if they're a sign of weakness. But your emotions are not the enemy; they are guides. They reveal your deeper needs and desires. Emotional freedom comes when you stop seeing your emotions as something to fix or suppress and start seeing them as part of your authentic experience. By embracing your emotions, even the difficult ones, you gain a deeper understanding of yourself and develop a compassionate relationship with all parts of you.

When you live in emotional freedom, you no longer need external validation to feel secure. You stop seeking approval from others and instead turn inward for the answers. This doesn't mean you stop caring about relationships or other people's feelings,it means you stop relying on them to define your worth. The only person who can truly validate you is you. Emotional freedom means knowing that you are enough exactly as you are, without needing anyone else's permission or approval.

Another crucial element of emotional freedom is **setting boundaries**. Boundaries are not walls meant to keep people out; they are a way to honor and protect your emotional space. They are a declaration of what you need to feel safe, respected, and valued. When you set boundaries from a place of emotional freedom, you're not afraid of how others will react, because you trust that honoring yourself is the most important thing you can do.

Living as your authentic self also means embracing **vulnerability**. Vulnerability is often misunderstood as weakness, but in reality, it is the birthplace of connection, creativity, and true courage. When you allow yourself to be vulnerable,whether that means expressing your true feelings, asking for help, or admitting that you don't have all the answers,you open the door to deeper, more meaningful relationships. You stop hiding behind masks and start showing up fully as yourself, flaws and all. Vulnerability is where emotional freedom thrives, because it allows you to live openly and honestly, without fear of rejection.

One of the most empowering aspects of emotional freedom is the realization that you are not responsible for how others perceive or react to you. You cannot control how others interpret your actions, nor can you shape their opinions. What you can control is how you show up in the world. You can choose to live authentically, regardless of how others respond. This is where true emotional liberation lies,in the understanding that your worth is not tied to anyone else's approval.

Emotional freedom also invites you to **let go of perfectionism**. When you strive to be perfect, you're living under the illusion that you need to meet some unattainable standard in order to be worthy of love or success. But perfection is a myth, and chasing it only leads to frustration, burnout, and self-criticism. True freedom comes when you allow yourself to be human,to make mistakes, to learn, to grow, and to love yourself in the process.

Finally, embodying emotional freedom means living with **joy and curiosity**. It's about approaching life with a sense of wonder, rather than fear. When you stop trying to control every outcome and start trusting in your ability to handle whatever comes your way, life becomes an adventure. You allow yourself to take risks, follow your passions, and explore new possibilities without the constant fear of failure. Emotional freedom opens the door to a life of richness, meaning, and deep fulfillment.

Daily Rituals for Maintaining Emotional Freedom

To help you embody emotional freedom in your everyday life, here are a few simple yet powerful daily rituals. These practices are designed to help you stay connected to your authentic self and maintain the sense of freedom and peace that comes from living in alignment with who you truly are.

Step 1: Morning Intention Setting

- *Begin each day by setting an intention for how you want to show up in the world. This intention can be as simple as "I will honor my emotions today" or "I will trust myself in every decision I make." Setting an intention in the morning helps you stay connected to your emotional freedom throughout the day.*
- *Take a few deep breaths as you set your intention, and visualize yourself embodying that intention in different situations you may face.*

Step 2: Emotional Check-In

- *At some point during the day,whether it's during a lunch break or a quiet moment,take a few minutes to check in with your emotions. Ask yourself, "What am I feeling right now?" Don't try to change or fix the emotion, just acknowledge it.*
- *If the emotion is uncomfortable, offer yourself compassion. You might say, "It's okay that I'm feeling anxious," or "It's natural to feel*

disappointed." By acknowledging and accepting your emotions, you are practicing emotional freedom.

Step 3: Gratitude Reflection

- *At the end of each day, take a moment to reflect on something you are grateful for. This could be a meaningful conversation, a moment of joy, or even the opportunity to learn from a challenge.*
- *Write down one or two things that made you feel connected to yourself or others that day. Gratitude helps you stay grounded in the present moment and reminds you of the abundance in your life, no matter what challenges you're facing.*

Step 4: Setting Boundaries

- *Identify one area of your life where you need to set a boundary. It could be with your time, your energy, or your emotional space. Write down what that boundary looks like and why it is important to you.*
- *Commit to enforcing that boundary, even if it feels uncomfortable. Boundaries are a key part of maintaining emotional freedom because they help you protect your peace and well-being.*

Step 5: Letting Go of Perfection

- *Each day, practice letting go of perfection in one small way. This might mean giving yourself permission to make a mistake, to take a break, or to be less than "perfect" in a conversation or task.*
- *Remind yourself that perfection is not the goal, authenticity is. When you let go of the need to be perfect, you create space for growth, creativity, and deeper connections.*

Step 6: Evening Reflection on Vulnerability

- *At the end of the day, reflect on one moment where you allowed yourself to be vulnerable. Maybe it was asking for help, sharing your true feelings, or admitting that you didn't have all the answers.*
- *Celebrate that vulnerability as a sign of strength and emotional freedom. Each time you show up authentically, you reinforce the belief that you are enough just as you are.*

Embodying emotional freedom is about living fully and authentically, free from the need to hide, control, or perfect yourself. It's about trusting your emotions, setting boundaries, and letting go of the constant pressure to meet unrealistic expectations. Emotional freedom allows you to navigate life's challenges with grace, knowing that your worth is not tied to external validation or approval.

As you integrate these daily rituals into your life, you will find that emotional freedom becomes not just an idea, but a way of being. You will feel more connected to your true self, more confident in your decisions, and more open to the joys and challenges that life brings. This is the essence of living as your secure, authentic self,free to be exactly who you are, in every moment, without fear or hesitation.

CHAPTER 22

Cultivating a Secure Attachment Mindset

Long-Term Strategies for Security and Emotional Well-Being

At the core of our emotional well-being lies one powerful truth: the way we connect with others shapes the way we connect with ourselves. The more secure we feel in our relationships, the more grounded, confident, and emotionally stable we become. This sense of security, often referred to as "secure attachment," allows us to navigate life with ease, trusting that no matter what comes our way, we are safe, supported, and loved.

However, many of us did not grow up with the gift of secure attachment. For those who have experienced inconsistent or unhealthy connections, it can feel like emotional security is out of reach, something reserved for others. But here's the good news: a secure attachment mindset is something that can be developed and cultivated, no matter where you're starting from. It's a shift in perspective, a way of approaching life and relationships that creates a foundation for lasting emotional well-being.

To cultivate a secure attachment mindset, you must first understand what secure attachment looks and feels like. People with secure attachment trust both themselves and others. They feel safe being vulnerable, knowing that their needs will be met, and they trust that the people in their lives will respond with care and empathy. This sense of security doesn't mean they never experience fear or doubt,it means they have the tools to manage those emotions without being overwhelmed by them.

The foundation of a secure attachment mindset is **self-trust**. Before you can build healthy, secure relationships with others, you must first learn to trust yourself. This means trusting your emotions, your instincts, and your ability to handle whatever life brings. It means knowing that no matter what happens, you will take care of yourself. Self-trust is built through consistency,showing up for yourself day after day, in small and big ways, and proving to yourself that you are reliable.

One of the first steps to building self-trust is learning to **regulate your emotions**. People with secure attachment aren't free from anxiety or fear, but they know how to manage those feelings without letting them take over. This doesn't mean suppressing your emotions or pretending everything is fine. It means acknowledging what you're feeling and taking steps to soothe yourself in healthy ways. Simple practices like deep breathing, mindfulness, and journaling can help you stay grounded when emotions run high.

In addition to self-trust, cultivating a secure attachment mindset requires **open and honest communication**. People with secure attachment are not afraid to express their needs or set boundaries because they trust that doing so won't lead to rejection or abandonment. If you've grown up in an environment where emotional needs were met with neglect or criticism, speaking up for yourself might feel uncomfortable at first. But the more you practice, the easier it becomes. Clear communication creates deeper connections, allowing both you and the people in your life to feel seen and understood.

It's also important to recognize that **secure attachment is not about perfection**. No relationship,whether with yourself or others,is free from conflict, doubt, or difficulty. The key is how you handle those challenges. People with secure attachment don't shy away from conflict; they face it head-on, with curiosity and compassion. They understand that disagreements and misunderstandings are part of being human, and they approach these moments as opportunities for growth rather than threats to the relationship.

One of the most powerful strategies for cultivating a secure attachment mindset is learning to **challenge the negative beliefs** that keep you stuck in insecurity. If you struggle with anxious or avoidant attachment patterns, you might believe things like, "I'm not lovable," "People will leave me," or "I can't trust anyone." These beliefs are rooted in past experiences, not present reality. To cultivate a secure attachment mindset, you must actively work to challenge and reframe these beliefs.

Start by recognizing when these thoughts come up. When you catch yourself thinking, "I can't trust anyone," pause and ask yourself, "Is this thought based on my current reality, or is it a reflection of past wounds?" Then, challenge the thought by reminding yourself of times when trust was earned or given in your relationships. This practice helps you break free from old patterns and create a mindset rooted in trust, both for yourself and others.

Another key element of a secure attachment mindset is **self-compassion**. Often, the hardest person to be kind to is yourself. But self-compassion is essential for building emotional security because it teaches you that it's okay to make mistakes and that your worth isn't tied to being perfect. People with secure attachment forgive themselves easily and don't dwell on their shortcomings. They know that being human means being imperfect, and they embrace their flaws with kindness rather than judgment.

Self-compassion also helps you weather the storms of life without getting swept away. When you're able to treat yourself with kindness, you create an internal safety net that supports you through life's inevitable ups and downs. This inner security is the foundation of a secure attachment mindset. It allows you to face challenges with resilience, knowing that you have your own back no matter what.

In addition to self-compassion, **gratitude** plays a significant role in cultivating emotional security. When you focus on what's going well in your life, you shift your mindset from fear to abundance. Gratitude helps you see the goodness that already exists, even when things feel difficult. It grounds you in the present moment and reminds you that you are supported, even in small ways. Practicing gratitude daily rewires your brain to focus on security rather than scarcity, helping you cultivate a secure attachment mindset.

Building a Support System for Ongoing Growth

One of the most important aspects of cultivating a secure attachment mindset is surrounding yourself with a support system that encourages your growth. Healing and personal development don't happen in isolation. You need people in your life who see you, support you, and hold space for your continued journey toward security and well-being.

Here are steps to help you build a strong support system:

Step 1: Identify Your Support Needs

- *Start by reflecting on what you need from your support system. Are you looking for emotional encouragement, practical advice, or simply someone to listen without judgment? Write down what kind of support would feel most meaningful to you at this point in your journey.*
- *Consider the different areas of your life where you might need support: relationships, career, personal growth, or emotional well-being. Each area might require a different kind of support, so be specific about your needs.*

Step 2: Evaluate Your Current Relationships

- *Take an honest look at the people currently in your life. Are there individuals who consistently support your growth and emotional well-being? Are there relationships that drain your energy or contribute to insecurity?*

- *Make a list of the people who uplift you and the people who may be holding you back. This exercise helps you gain clarity about where you might need to set boundaries or invest more energy.*

Step 3: Expand Your Support Network

- *If you feel like you don't have enough support in certain areas of your life, think about ways to expand your network. This could mean joining a community group, finding a mentor, or seeking professional support like a therapist or coach.*
- *Surrounding yourself with people who share your values and are committed to personal growth will help reinforce your secure attachment mindset. Look for relationships that are built on mutual respect, trust, and emotional safety.*

Step 4: Practice Vulnerability

- *Building a support system requires vulnerability. This means being open about your needs, feelings, and experiences. Start by sharing something personal with someone you trust. It could be a fear, a dream, or a challenge you're facing.*
- *Notice how it feels to be vulnerable. Often, when you open up, you create deeper connections with*

others. Vulnerability invites others to support you in meaningful ways.

Step 5: Set Boundaries Where Needed

- *As you build your support system, it's crucial to set healthy boundaries. Boundaries protect your emotional well-being and ensure that your relationships are balanced and respectful.*
- *Identify any relationships where you need to set clearer boundaries. This might mean limiting your time with someone who drains your energy or being clear about what you need from a particular relationship.*

Step 6: Offer Support to Others

- *Secure attachment is a two-way street. Just as you need support, others in your life do as well. Take time to be there for the people who support you. Offer a listening ear, words of encouragement, or help when they need it.*
- *Building a strong support system is about mutual care and respect. When you invest in others, they are more likely to invest in you.*

Cultivating a secure attachment mindset is a lifelong journey of self-discovery, trust, and emotional growth. It's about shifting from a mindset of fear, insecurity, and scarcity to one rooted in trust, compassion, and abundance. By developing self-trust, practicing vulnerability, setting boundaries, and building a strong support system, you create a foundation of emotional security that supports your long-term well-being.

As you continue on this path, remember that cultivating security doesn't mean you won't face challenges. It means you will have the tools and inner resources to navigate those challenges with grace and resilience. The more you practice these strategies, the more natural they will become, and over time, you will find yourself moving through life with a deep sense of emotional freedom and confidence.

Your relationships will begin to reflect this newfound security, as you attract people who support and uplift you. And most importantly, your relationship with yourself will transform into one of trust, compassion, and unwavering belief in your own worth. This is the essence of a secure attachment mindset a mindset that allows you to live fully, love deeply, and experience the richness of life with an open heart.

CONCLUSION

As we come to the end of this chapter, I invite you to take a moment and think about the progress you've made. The path to emotional freedom isn't one you stumble upon by accident. You've chosen it, and it's taken real courage to face your fears, explore the parts of yourself you may have hidden away, and push through the layers of pain and self-doubt. In peeling those back, you've uncovered something truly special: your authentic self.

This journey hasn't been about perfection or avoiding the tough parts of life. Instead, it's about finding a sense of inner security, building trust in yourself, and handling life's ups and downs with a sense of calm. Emotional freedom doesn't mean you'll never feel fear, sadness, or anger again. But now, when those feelings come, they don't control you. You've learned how to face them with compassion and understanding, without letting them take over.

You've discovered how to manage emotional triggers, rebuild self-trust, and form meaningful connections. You now see setbacks not as failures, but as moments to grow. Along the way, you've also recognized how important it is to set boundaries that protect your emotional health. These lessons are the foundation for a life where you can be yourself fully, without holding back.

Take some time to ask yourself: How do you feel different from when you first began? What have you learned about your emotions, your relationships, and yourself? What strengths have surfaced that you didn't notice before? Reflecting on these questions helps you see that healing and growth are not abstract ideas,they're part of your lived experience, and you're already living them.

As you move forward, there are a few core lessons to keep close to heart. They'll guide you as you continue creating a life built on security, authenticity, and emotional well-being.

Trust Yourself Trusting yourself is the foundation of emotional freedom. This trust grows when you consistently show up for yourself whether that's by honoring your feelings, setting boundaries, or following your gut. It doesn't mean you'll never slip up; it means you believe in your ability to handle whatever life throws your way. Self-trust helps you make choices that align with your values and approach relationships with confidence. When you trust yourself, you're no longer swayed by others' opinions you're rooted in your own inner wisdom.

Be Open to Vulnerability Emotional freedom comes from the courage to be vulnerable. Sharing your deepest thoughts, emotions, or fears allows for real connection,with yourself and with others. Vulnerability isn't a sign of weakness; it shows that you're strong enough to be open, even if there's a chance you could be misunderstood or hurt. The more you allow yourself to be vulnerable, the more you'll see how it strengthens your relationships and adds real meaning to your life.

Set Healthy Boundaries Clear boundaries are essential for emotional freedom. They're not about pushing people away,they're about protecting your emotional and mental well-being. Boundaries help you engage in relationships from a place of wholeness, not from depletion. They're a sign of self-respect and reflect your commitment to living authentically. Going forward, continue honoring your boundaries with care, knowing that by doing so, you're nurturing your growth.

Embrace Setbacks as Growth Opportunities One of the most freeing parts of emotional growth is realizing that setbacks are part of the process, not failures. Whenever you experience a setback, like falling into old habits or doubting yourself, you now have the tools to recover with kindness. Each setback reinforces what you've learned and allows for deeper healing. Growth isn't a straight line,it comes in layers, and setbacks are just part of the learning process.

Nurture Secure Relationships Your emotional freedom will flourish in relationships where you feel safe, supported, and valued. Continue seeking and maintaining connections that are built on trust, mutual respect, and emotional safety. These are the relationships that will uplift you and support your freedom. Surround yourself with people who see and appreciate the real you, and remember, you deserve relationships that honor your authentic self.

Practice Daily Self-Compassion The work of emotional freedom is ongoing. There will be moments of doubt and fear along the way, and during those times, the best thing you can offer yourself is compassion. Self-compassion counters self-criticism and judgment, creating a nurturing space for ongoing healing. By practicing kindness toward yourself, even when things don't go as planned, you allow your growth to continue.

Final Thoughts Living with emotional freedom is an act of deep self-love. It means showing up for yourself every day, trusting your inner voice, and taking care of your emotional needs. It's about no longer letting fear, doubt, or others' expectations hold you back. Instead, you move through life with confidence and peace, knowing that you are enough, just as you are.

There will be times when old patterns or doubts creep in, moments when you question whether you're capable. In those times, I encourage you to remember what you've learned. You already have everything you need within you,strength, wisdom, and compassion. Trust in that.

Emotional freedom isn't about living without challenges. It's about knowing you have the resilience and tools to face them. It's about showing up fully for life, open to both joy and pain, without needing to guard yourself against either. It's about living with curiosity, courage, and love,for yourself and for those who matter most to you.

As you continue on this journey, be proud of how far you've come. It's not easy, but it's one of the most rewarding things you can do. You're creating a life that aligns with who you truly are, where you can express yourself fully and build relationships that bring real meaning and fulfillment.

So, keep going. Keep trusting yourself. Keep embracing vulnerability. Keep setting boundaries that support your well-being. Keep seeing setbacks as opportunities for growth. Keep nurturing the relationships that uplift you. And above all, keep practicing self-compassion, day by day.

You are capable of living with emotional freedom. You're already well on your way. The path will continue to unfold in ways you can't predict, but each step brings you closer to the life of peace and fulfillment you deserve.

This is your life. Live it with freedom. Live it with love. Live it as your true, authentic self.